BLACK TUESDAY
AND
AFTER

BLACK TUESDAY AND AFTER

Basetty Narsing Rao

B.Com., L.L.B., Hyderabad, A.P.

Edited by

L.S. Ramaiah

Uni. Librarian (Retd.)

CIEFL, Hyderabad, A.P.

Reference Press

4831/24, Ansari Road
Darya Ganj
New Delhi-110 002
Phone : 23260807
Fax : 23274173
E-mail: essess@del3vsnl.net.in

First Published 2004

ISBN : 81-88583-67-7

Price : Rs. 325/-

Published by :

Reference Press

4831/24, Ansari Road, Darya Ganj,
New Delhi - 110 002
Phone : 23260807
Fax : 23274173

Printed at :
Print Line

FOREWORD

I made a modest an effort to elucidate the collapse of the twin towers of the World Trade Centre in New York city, and the consequential fight against terrorism all over the Globe.

I offer my heart-felt condolences to the families of victims killed in a very horrific and tragic incident in the whirlpool of fire of World Trade Center. This was the first time that the U.S. has felt the lash of terrorists on its home land and declared war against terrorism. Though the U.S. and allied forces succeeded in driving out Taliban forces from Afghanistan and devastated the Al-Qaeda's training and organisational infrastructure they could not capture the ring leaders who were behind the conspiracy to maelstorm the World Trade Center even after thirty months of frantic search. With eerie silence the whole world is flustered and flummoxed on the disappearance of Laden and Omar from the main scene of Afghanistan.

In this book I tried to narrate the day to day important events that took place in the World from September 11, 2001 to the end of March 2004 to combat terrorism and the fall of Taliban ruled Afghanistan to the U.S. and allied forces.

In this endeavour, I never forget the help rendered by Mrs. Kameswari and Miss. Vanitha of Infologic Systems. I am also thankful to Shri K. Sudhir who after going through the entire script encouraged me to bring it out in the form of a book. I am happy to record my grateful thanks to Mr. L.S. Ramaiah who has taken pains to edit the text and update it here and there. My thanks are also due to Mr. Sumit Sethi, Proprietor and Manager of the Reference Press, New Delhi who has designed and printed the book with elegence.

I may be pardoned of any error committed unknowingly.

Basetty Narsing Rao

FOREWORD

I made a modest an effort to elucidate the collapse of the twin towers of the World Trade Centre in New York city, and the consequential fight against terrorism all over the world.

I offer my heart-felt condolences to the families of victims killed in a very horrific and tragic incident in the [illegible] of the World Trade Center. This was the first time that the U.S. has felt the lash of terrorists on its home land and declared war against terrorism. Though the U.S. and allied forces succeeded in driving out Taliban forces from Afghanistan and devastated the Al-Qaeda's training and organisational infrastructure they could not capture the top leaders who were behind the conspiracy to devastate the World Trade Centre even after three months of frantic search. With certainty, the whole world is flustered and dismayed on the disappearance of Laden and Omar from the [illegible] scene of Afghanistan.

In this book I tried to narrate the day to day important events that took place in the World from September 11, 2001 to the end of March 2002 to combat terrorism and the fall of Taliban ruled Afghanistan to the U.S. and allied forces.

In this endeavour, I never forget the help rendered by Miss Kameswari and Miss. Vanitha of Infologic Systems. I am most thankful to Shri K. Sastry who after going through the entire script encouraged me to bring it out in the form of a book. I am happy to record my grateful thanks to Mr. I. S. Ramaiah who has taken pains to edit the text and update it here and there. My thanks are also due to Mr. Sumit Sethi, Proprietor and Manager of the [illegible] Press, New Delhi who has designed and printed the book with elegance.

I will be pardoned of any some committed unknowingly.

[illegible]

Dedicated to the memory of Men, Women and Children killed in the terrorist attacks all over the World

CONTENTS

1

NEW YORK CITY

The city of New York is situated at a confluence of waterways which include the Atlantic ocean, the East River, and the Hudson River, with an abundance of coastline, deep channels, it is an ideal port and a harbour well protected from the open sea. As a matter of fact, the city of New York is on Manhattan Island.

The first recorded sighting of the area which is now known as New York was in the year 1524 by Giovanni da Verrazano, an Italian explorer in the employ of the king of France. It was after another eighty-five years that is in 1609, an Englishman exploring on behalf of the Dutch Government landed on Manhattan and claimed it for Holland.

On the Southern tip of Manhattan, a handful of European settlers spent their winter in 1613 and left the place in the spring. Then in 1624, permanent settlers sent by the Dutch West India Company visited again to the Southern tip, built a Fort, which they named as Fort Amsterdam and established a settlement called *Nieuw Amsterdam*. In 1626 Peter Minuit, a Dutch colonial official bought the island for twenty-four dollars from the Algonquin Indians. The scarcely populated area survived for next twenty-three years. Mr. Peter Stuyvesant became the Governor of the New Amsterdam in 1647 and from then on under his leadership the town began to prosper quickly.

As the time passed, the Englishmen acquired strongholds throughout the American colonies and established settlements in 1607 in James town, Virginia in 1620, in Plymouth and Massachusetts latter. In between 1652 and 1664 the Dutch settlers and the Englishmen engaged in slew of small skirmishes. Finally in 1664 English warships cruised into the harbour and forced Mr. Stuyvesant to surrender the New Amsterdam to the realm of English. The Dutch, however, regained the colony, but in a treaty of peace relinquished it to the English, where upon the town was renamed as New York.

The population of the New Amsterdam (renamed as New York,) which was one thousand in 1647, swelled to seven thousand by 1700. Particularly during the revolutionary times of 18th century, New York became an important center of the British. In January 1785, after the revolution it was declared as Capital City of the United States. Within a year the US capital was shifted to Philadelphia but that did not restrain the New York City to grow wildly. By 1800 the population of the city increased to sixty thousand and claimed the distinction as the largest city in the newly formed the United States of America, a position it has never relinquished.

Fascinated by the fast development of New York there were floods of immigrants in the 19th century from Germany, Ireland, China, Italy, Russia and other Eastern European countries creating ethnic enclaves that still exist. By the end of 20th century there was mass exodus of population from Israel, India, Japan and from many other countries of the world.

From its inception, New York is faced with troubles of ever growing population, resulting in unbearable traffic, crime, racial and ethnic conflicts, pollution, filth, drugs and unbearable high cost of living. It, however, claims the greatest of American dreams with myriad sky scrappers as if to pierce the sky, the Statue of Liberty, day and night traffic through out the year welcoming new comers to America's shore, the Great White way ablaze with the theoretical marquees, Rockefeller center at Christmas Central Park in the spring and the graceful expanse of the George Washington bridge spanning the serene Hudson River. Besides, the city of New

York is also comprised with numerous neighborhoods, marvelous parks, great history, glorified culture, and its high spirited people.

Whether one is a native of New York, an immigrant or a casual visitor it is not only the city of light but also the city of life, which normally never sleeps, bustling late into the night on any day of the week, traffic normally busy at all hours.

2

COLLAPSE OF THE TWIN TOWERS OF THE WORLD TRADE CENTER

WORLD TRADE CENTRE

The World Trade Centre often called simply the WTC is housed in the twin sky scrapers built (1968-1973) in New York city by the port authority of New York and N. Jersexy and designed by the architects Minoru Yamasaki and Emery Roth and the structural Engineering firm of skilling Helle, Christian son and Robinson:

Every characteristic of these immense Towers places them in a unique category; they are 110 stories of 411 m (1, 350 ft) high making them second in height only to the SEARS TOWERS in Chicago; they comprise 1.2 million m (13 million ft) of office space and the total building cost amounted to 750 million dollars.

The structural system, known as a braced tubular cantilever is a form of skyscraper construction that was developed in the 1960's but actually represents modern variant of that used in the EIFFEL TOWER adapted to extremely high buildings. The problem in the construction of all large framed structures is to render them rigid against the force of the wind.

This task is accomplished in the WTC towers by making each wall a rigid truss and joining the four trusses of the corners.

The result is a continuous tube of square section that results the bending and shearing forces of the wind, through the rigidity of its outer walls. The Towers have elicited recurring controversy over their architectural design, their location, their size and the consumption of energy necessary to maintain a stable internal environment. Their only feature that is beyond dispute is the advanced technology of their supporting structure.

When the world trade centre with its 1,340 foot high twin towers opened in 1974, it changed the scene of skyline. The 110 story monolithic towers designed by Minoru Yamasaki and Emery Roth & Sons were the tallest buildings in Manhattan and the second tallest buildings in the world. They also occupy the eminence of the world's fastest elevators housing one of the New York's most spectacularly sited restaurants, real estate agents, custom brokers and all other interests related to international trade. Added to all these adjectives the establishment of world trade centre gave a new birth of lower Manhattan.

The material scooped for the basements of the two massive and majestic towers created a twentythree acre landfill along the Hudson river. The World Trade Centre after its completion was leased by its owner Port Authority of New York and New Jersey for 99 years. The grand and sublime 110 story structures became a symbol of glory of the United States with cream of nationals of eighty countries engaging themselves in international trade and gave boast to American's economy.

It was beyond the imagination of anybody, more so of the citizens of the US that the massive and majestic 110 story twin towers of the World Trade Center will one day collapse like a pack of cards.

On the fateful day of Tuesday the eleventh of September 2001 at 8.42 a.m. in one of the most audacious attacks ever made against the United States, the suspected hijackers Marwan Al Shehi, Fayez Rasheed Ahmed Hussain Al Qadi Bamihammad, Mohald Alshehri, Hamza Alghamdi and Ahmed Alghamdi seized control of the United Airlines Flight 175 and slammed into the Northern

Tower of the World Trade Center in New York. Before anybody could recover from the shock another batch consisting of Waleed Al shehri, Wali Al Shehri, Mohammad Atta, Abdul Aziz Aloman and Satam Al Suqami hijacked a second American Airlines Flight 11 and slammed into the second tower and destroyed the World Trade Center completely at 9.00 am with an interval of just 18 minutes.

The massive structures of the World Trade Center engulfed in fire ball of flames crumbled like a movie set was unbelievable and beyond expression. No one in real life could have witnessed a more heart rending and horrific scene than desperate men and women trying to escape from the rising flames jumping fatally from the high floors of the 110-story tower.

The island city of New York laid of longitudinally, fairly cosmopolitan culture, the city that keep awake round the clock accommodating and sometimes grudging their transplaned residents, financial capital and primary trade center of their respected countries experienced horrific inexplicable spasms of fear, disgust, sadness, anguish and anger on the 11th of September 2001. The Americans were stunned into disbelief. It was the greatest shock of their lives. They felt pain in the subtlest part of their existence. They thought what hit them was no more terrorism. It was a sudden war declared against the US even against the humanity, against dignity and against civilization. The magnificent and disdainful towers which never learnt to stoop were engulfed in the fierce flames and reduced into ashes. The 110 story towers of the World Trade Center have gone. About 50,000 people from eighty countries work at the Trade Center and the two hijack planes that slammed the World Trade Center were carrying a total of 156 people. It is feared that about 3000 have either died or missing in the above havoc. The complexity of this kind of attack claimed the lives of 300 US fire fighters too.

There is no one who has not been impressed by the meticulousness of the planning the all round expertise and superb skills that made the terror strikes in New York and Washington so lethal. Whoever planned, it was sure to feel elevated by the way every thing changed in the world on that day. Naturally, they will feel inspired to strike again and they are sure to have many more trained experts waiting for orders. Some reports suggested that the core groups of attacks with advanced training has more than 1000 members. Perhaps no more than 30 of them were sacrificed in America.

The terrorists who destroyed the World Trade Center knew well that it could be seen as a symbol of many things, even of American virility but in actual fact it was to the American finance what the Pentagon is to American military. Due to the terrorists atrocity and their unique barbaric and cowardly act, the World Trade Center, which was symbol of pride of the US has completely vanished from the scene reminding, the fact that terrorists are no respecters of the borders and their hearts are not made of muscles, but of mud.

The twin towers of the World Trade Center, the most visible landmark of the US have gone. The 110 story cousins collapsed. They hit the Pentagon, which is the symbol of the American military might. The US President George Bush had to be hidden for a day and in fact the US had to be suspended virtually as a Nation.

The World Trade Center was leased by its owner, the Port authority of New York and New Jersey. The New York developer who led the group that bought a ninetynine year lease of the World Trade Center expressed his determination to help rebuild the complex and the neighbouring office tower that also collapsed. The developer Mr.Larry Silverstein said that a memorial for the victims should also be developed on the site and should not give the terrorist the victory that they sought.

The Foreign and Defence Minister of India who came to New York on the first of October paid tributes to the people who died in the terrorist attack and handed over two silver Urns, one containing water from nine sacred Indian rivers and the second containing soil from different parts of India to the Mayor of New York city, Rudy Gluliani. He requested the Mayor that "whenever you build a memorial for World Trade Centre victims please use this water and soil in its foundation as a token of our fight against Terrorism". Thanking him Gluliani said "we will definitely use this as a symbol of friendship between the United States and India.

It has taken three months for the US to extinguish the fire caused by the terrorists attack on theWorld Trade Centre.

The glory of the twin massive spires of New York departed leaving the hearts of every American with a great deal of poignancy and profound sorrow.

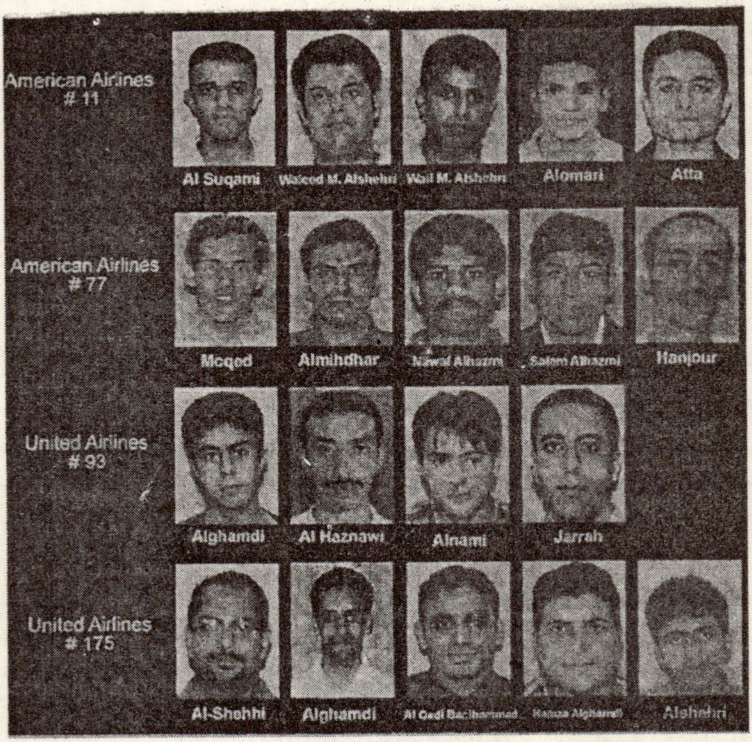

Source : The US Department of Justice on Thursday released the names and pictures of hijack suspects on the flights that crashed into the WTC, Pentagon and in Pennsylvania - Reuters

BRIEF HISTORY OF PENTAGON

The Pentagon is located in Arlignton, Va, across the Potomac River from washington, DC is a five story, five sided building that is Head Quarters for the departments of Defence and of the Army, the Navy and the Air force. Designed by architect G.E. Bergstorm with the intent to conserve structural steel, which was in short supply during World War II, this building was completed in January, 1943 after 16 months of round the clock work. It consists of five Pentagon shaped building that form concentric rings joined by corridor. The Pentagon, having approximately 343740 m (3,700,000 ft) of office space also has its own fire department police force, radio and television station and telephone exchange.

ATTACK ON PENTAGON

Pentagon is the mighty military head-quarters and nerve center of the United States. On the 11th September of Tuesday, Khalid Al-Midhar, Majed Moqued, Nawaz Alhamzi, Salem Alhamzi and Hanjour suspected to have hijacked the American, Airlines Flight 77 and gouged a hole in the Pentagon building at 9.30 am resulting a portion of one side of the five sided structure collapsed.

For all the technological prowess and military might the United States did not visualize the attack and proved beyond doubt that this was stunning the American Security Intelligence failure. As there was total failure of the US intelligence, it took measures to reassess the intelligence operations of the country to give the US spies more discretion to conduct covert operations to hunt out the terrorists. It looks funny and appeared to be like a fairy tale that a country developing a science fictional missile defence umbrella was humbled by a dozen and half men carrying only knives and card board cutters.

The objects targeted for these attacks were strategically determined to achieve maximum impact. Destroying the twin towers located in the economic capital not just of the USA but perhaps even of the entire world was part of the terrorists capability of disturbing the American economy by ramification, the international economy at their foundations. Attacking the Defence Department and the U.S. Army Head Quarters in the Pentagon building was to convey a parallel message that regardless of the USA military and technological supermacy the terrorists can reach the very nerve center of its strategic capacities.

Mohammad Afroz who was arrested by Maharashtra Police in the month of November confessed a startling couspiracy of Al-Qaeda to attack Britain, Australia and Indian Parliament House. Significantly Afroz learnt flying from the same school which trained Al-Qaeda militants who hijacked and crashed four aircraft in the US on September, 11. The police have also recovered a passport from the house of Afroz at Trombay which carries visas of the US, Australia and Britain.

The US authorities who were groping in the dark to know the hidden enemy got two black boxes from the plane that demolished the West End of the Pentagon.

CRASH IN PENNSYLVANIA

As if all the misdeeds done at the World Trade Center and the Pentagon were not enough the suspected terrorists consisting of Ahmed Alhaznir, Ahmed Alnami, Ziad Samir Jarrah and Saeed Alghamdi took control of the United Airlines Flight 93 enroute from New York, New Jersey to San Francisco on the black Tuesday and got crashed about 130 km South East of Pittsburgh killing all the 45 people aboard.

Mrs. Barbarloson, wife of Solicitor General Theudoreloson, who was travelling in the above plane told her husband over the cellphone that the hijackers were not carrying fire arms but were armed with knives and card board cutters, herded the passengers and crew including the pilot towards the back of the plane and told them that there was more than one hijackers.

It was really surprised to see how the world's mightiest fighting force with advanced technology succumbed to the stratagem of few scamps in the name of religion.

3

FICTIONS AND PREDICTIONS

PROPHECY OF NOSTRADAMUS

Nobody imagined or dreamt that the massive and majestic 110 story twin towers will one day, become the target of some scamps sullen and saddled with religious fervor.

Ofcourse, the Nostradamus prediction comes true. Born in 1503, Michel de Nostradame better known as Nostradamus a famous 16th century French seer, had said in the prophecies that a turban man from the middle-east would come and plunge the world into the Third World War.

In his prediction Nostradamus referred to a great city in the new world of America near 45 degrees latitude being the first target of the Third World War. Experts had said it could only be New York. He says :-

"The sky will burn at forty five degrees
fire approaches the great new city.
By fire he will destroy their city,
a cold and cruel heart,
blood will pour,
mercy to none."

Nostradamus also spoke of a third Anti-Christ who is more hideous than all the other combined. Some say that it is Iraq's Saddam Hussain while others say that he has not yet appeared. But it could be Bin Laden. He says.

"He will come from the Middle – East,

Out of the country of greater Arabia,

Shall be born a strong master,

He will enter Europe wearing a blue turban,

He will be the terror of mankind,

Never more horror."

Here, Nostradamus says that a man from the greater Arabia will lead his forces on an invasion through the Europe. This invasion will begin a Third World War that will be far worse than all the other wars put together.

When will all this take place? In one quatrain Nostradamus gives an exact date in which the war will be well underway.

In century 10, Quatrain 72, Nostradamus refers to the millennium

"In the year 1999 and seven months (July),

From the sky will come the great king of terror,

He will bring back to life the king of Mongols,

before and after war reigns."

The prophecy of Nostradamus is that the war will begin shortly before the year 1999. It will last for 27 years. The war will be so terrible that the world will come face to face with final annihilation.

The prediction of the seer implies that the countries engaged in the war might use nuclear weapons. Though the prophecy of the seer pose frightening picture, he however, provided some hope saying that the Third World War will end as a result of alliance not expected.

"When those of the Northern pole are united,

in the east will be great fear and dread......,

one day the great two leaders will be friends,

their great powers will be seen to grow.

The new land will be at the height of its power,

to the man of blood the number is reported."

Nostradamus viewed America as new land and the countries of the North pole could be Russia and the United States.

In recent years after breakdown of Communism in U.S.S.R, we are seeing that increasing friendship between Russia and the United States.

Fictions

Shrewd scientists all over the world sometimes turn fictions into facts. The terrorists with limited purpose and resources might pick up the ideas from these stories of fiction and films and turn them into facts as was seen in New York and Washington.

It was just about two decades ago that Lapierre, along with Larry Collins, had painted a scenario that would sound eerily similar to what happened in Manhattan on Tuesday morning. In that bestseller *The Fifth Horseman*, Lapierre and Collins had spun a fearsome yarn of Palestinian terrorists, backed by Gadhafi, planting a nuclear bomb in a New York basement. Gadafi then asked the U.S. President to get the Israelis to withdraw from Jerusalem by a deadline or he would detonate the nuke and write off Manhattan.

Tom Clancy came even closer to the World Trade Center story in his *Executive Orders*, built around the unlikely plot of a U.S. Japanese war. A Boeing 747 pilot, distraught at having lost a family member in the war, crashes his (empty) plane into Capital Hill while the Vice-President is being sworn in, causing a really high powered VIP carnage.

Tom Clancy indeed it is who should be worrying, if whoever planned attacks could be one of his avid readers. In his *Sum of all Fear*, he had also painted another similar sounding picture. Palestinian terrorists extract plutonium from a nuclear bomb, the Israelis lost during the Yom Kipur war, re-engineer it into a boosted fission device and explode it at the Superbowl attended by the usual retinue of VIPs and celebrities. The added twist was that they create the impression that somehow the Soviets were behind it.

If these are not enough, there was *Red Dragon* by Thomas Harris (better known as the author of *The Silence of the Lambs and Hanniabal*). The suspects are the usual ones, the Palestinains. This time they pack a nuke in a dirigible, take off from New York to fly over the packed Yankee stadium to vapourise, what else, but the Superbowl. This kind of mass urban terrorism has been a lasting spy-fiction fantasy and the terrorists could have picked up the idea from any of these.

Sometimes fictions are turned into facts and the predictions go unnoticed.

4

STATEMENT OF PRESIDENT GEORGE W. BUSH

The terrorist attacks quickly spread fear and chaos in the United States and President Bush was taken to a secret Nebraska location and the White House and the State Departments were also evacuated. The blow by blow attack forced the US to shut down all of its airports and all the US bound flights diverted to Canada.

The terror attacks on the World Trade Center and the Pentagon had wide ranging effect on economy in the world. The Americans were dignified in their grief and grindy purposeful placing the President Bush in the tightest of spots.

President Bush said in Sarasota Florida, "today we have had a National tragedy" and ordered a full-scale investigation "to hunt down the folks who committed this act". After consulting his top Security Advisors, President Bush asserted that "The hidden enemy" would not be allowed to hide for ever". While leading the Memorial Service in Washington President Bush emphasized his tough stand saying that the enemy has chosen the timing of the first shots of the war but the US would dictate when and how it ended and declared a State Emergency.

He also warned Pakistan against giving assistance to the terrorists. The stern warning given by President Bush that "we do not distinguish between terrorists and those who harbour them will be punished," placed Pakistan in a predicament as Bin Laden was in next door of Afghanistan. President Bush in Camp David again identified Bin Laden as the "prime suspect" who could not hide" and told the US troops to get ready to retaliate for Americas worst terror attack.

After an hour long meeting with the US Defence Secretary, Donald Rumsfeld with regard to the military plans for mobilizing reservists to beef up domestic defences against terrorism, President Bush at times raising his voice in anger told reporters, "I want justice, and want Osmana dead or alive". He further declared that "we are going to find those evil doers, those barbaric people who attacked our country and we are going to hold the people who housed them accountable" and made clear that the Taliban should take his statement seriously. At the joint session of the Congress on the 20th of September President Bush asked his country people to prepare for a long "war on terrorism" and reiterated again that the Taliban should turn over Bin Laden and his leading followers or share their fate. President Bush said all evidence gathered so far pointed to Bin Laden and Al-Quaida organization and responsible for the 11th of September attack.

Displaying the shield of George Howard, a New York police officer, who died trying to save lives at the World Trade Center, President Bush offered friends and foes a steely symbol of resolve and determination. He said "I will not forget this wound to our country or those who inflicted it". "I will not yield, "I will not rest" "I will not relent" in waging this struggle for the freedom and security of the American people to the loud cheers of the Congress, the cabinet, military leaders, foreign dignitaries and representatives of New York fire and police departments.

President Bush in his weekly radio address made it clear on the 29th of September that America wage war "wherever terrorist hide or run or plan". We did not seek this conflict, but we will end it. "America will act deliberately and decisively and the cause of freedom will prevail" he said. "Our war an terror will be much broader than the battle fields and beach heads of the past". President Bush said, "some victories will be won outside the public view in tragedies avoided and threats eliminated other victories will be clear to all".

The Bush administration was, therefore, compelled and constrained to consolidate the consensus after the terrorist attack that the fight against terror must include action against the nations who support terrorist groups.

The above attitude and awareness of America was needed long back, when India times without number called upon it to condemn terrorist attacks unleashed by Pakistan in Jammu & Kashmir.

5

OSMANA BIN LADEN – THE PRIME SUSPECT

President Bush declared that the Saudi dissident, Osmana Bin Laden is the prime suspect in the unprecedented and horrific attack on the United States for its support of Israel. Three weeks before the attack Bin Laden warned that he and his followers would carry out an unprecedented attack on the US interests for it support of Israel. Experts in the US who studied Bin Laden's track record of deadly attacks on the US targets combined with the unparalleled networks and deep war chest made Bin Laden the prime suspect in the strikes on New York and Washington. He was already alleged for master minding the 1998 twin bombings of the US Embassies in East Africa that killed more than 200 people.

Osama Bin Laden 42 was born in Jeddah, the 12th child of the construction magnate, Mohammad Bin Aaud Bin Laden whose assets were once valued at five billion dollars. One of the 58 children by many wives, Osman's connections were forged through his father who served sincerely the Saudi Royal family. His mother was living in Syria and he talked to his mother over the telephone on the 10th September and reported to have told her that he could not meet her there because something big was imminent that would end their communication for a long time.

Bin Laden's 51- year old half brother, Yeslam Bin Laden is

a Geneva based businessman and got his Swiss citizenship in May 2001. His Saudi Investments Company established in 1980 is based in the picturesque lake side city. He expressed his deepest feeling of sorrow over the attacks on the World Trade Center and said that he has not met his younger brother Osmana Bin Laden since 1981 and does not agree with his policies.

According to Mr. Brain Fyfield Shayler, British teacher who taught Laden English at an elite Saudi Arabian school said that Bin Laden was a quiet and shy pupil and behaved well, did all his work on time and particularly was not religious. He remembers Laden as quiet, retiring and rather shy and was very courteous, more so than any of others in his class. Laden, son of a wealthy industrialist joined 30 boys in Mr. Fyfield's class at the Al-Thaghr school in Jeddah during 1968-69.

Prince Bandar Bin Sultan, Saudi Ambassador to the USA said that the family members of Laden are lovely human beings who have suffered a lot because of Laden's activities. They are all well educated, successful businessmen involved in a lot of charities. He said further that Laden had an unhappy childhood and flipped over religion and was a black sheep of the family in a way, and for a while they thought his religious leanings were of a positive thinking. It is just something flipped inside of him.

Unable to bear the terrorist activities and criticism of the Royal family, the Saudi Arabia withdrew the citizenship of Laden in 1994. However, the Saudi Arabia is protecting the relatives of Laden just as the same as all other citizens. Prince Nayaf Bin Abdul Aziz said that his kingdom has not withdrawn Saudi nationalist from several children of Laden who are living in Saudi Arabia, who do not have any dealing with their father. As a matter of fact, after the September 11 attack the 24 member of Laden family flown out of the US with the co-ordination of FBI.

Laden, the Saudi born lives in Afghanistan as a "guest" of the Taliban militia since 1996 and leads Al-Qaida Terrorist Organization. He is surrounded himself with a tight circle of mostly

Saudi and Egyptian lieutenants who run a complicated world-wide network.

Ayman Zawahiri was physician and leader of the Islamic Jehad organization, which has claimed responsibility for a series of terrorist attacks on Egypt. Three years ago Zawahiri formally merged his group with Al-Qaida creating a movement that called itself the world Islamic front for "Jehad" against Jesus and crusaders. Mr. Mohammad serves as a military Commander. Abu Zubaydah a Saudi, Shaik Salid suspected pay master for the September 11 attack are the field commanders, who are loyal to Laden and responsible for running the Laden show.

According to Russian information Bin Laden had atleast 55 bases or offices in Afghanistan earlier with over 13,000 men ranging from Arabs to Pakistanis. In addition to the above, Laden is having 3500 fundamentalist Pakistanis as soldiers, diplomats and advisers to run the Taliban movement.

Trainees in terrorist camps in Afghanistan learned how to assassinate, commit sabotage, unleash poisons and build explosives, testified a convicted terrorist collaborator Ahmed Ressam. He further revealed his training for chemical attacks included watching his "Chief " place, a dog in a box and took the box with cyanide and sulfuric acid. It took the dog about four minutes to die. In regard to targets he said America as enemy of Islam. Ressam told further those at the camp with him in 1999 learned how to place cyanide near buildings as intake to kill as many people as they could without endangering themselves. Ressam told the authorities that while at the camp he learned how to mix poisons with oil substances and smear them on the door knobs so those who touched them would be killed by toxin coursing through their blood.

In the heart of London a mosque is found to be the center of terrorist activities and a common link between the perpetrators of the September 11 terror strikes in the U.S. and Laden. French intelligence calls the capital "Londonistan" because myriad Al-Qaida suspects take shelter here between trips to Afghanistan.

After nearly of a month investigation from the date of terror attack, the FBI had uncovered that some of the hijackers did not have a clue about the nature of their mission. The investigation revealed that only about six terrorists had the knowledge of the mission and their imminent death. The investigators believe that such a large group of people could be assembled to carry out the operation that must have taken months, if not years of planning without a leak or break in their ranks.

According to the former President Bill Clinton, the agenda of Laden is to bring down Saudi Arabia monarchy, replacing with a Palestinian State, installing regimes similar to Afghanistan fundamentalist Taliban in Arab nations and driving the U.S. out of the Middle-East.

Palestinian Foreign Minister Farook Gadomi said in the UAE capital Laden's pronouncements are simply aimed winning sympathies and support of Arabs and Islamic masses and Palestinians have nothing to do with him. From the above statements, it could be gauged that Laden is not interested either in Palestinia nor Kashmir. He is interested in theocracy and rule Afghanistan as a dictator. President Musharraf was quoted as telling the "*U.S.A. Today*" and CBS Television, "Get Mullah Omar and Osama wont be able to operate. He will be on the run! He also doubted the ability of Taliban to muster enough force to defeat the U.S. troops when a ground assault in Afghanistan is finally launched. "It could be over in one day if you take out Omar and his leadership" he said.

The U.S. has released the much awaited videotape of Laden on the 13th December,2001 apparently recounting plans for the September,11 attack on the U.S. and said his comments in Afghanistan were proof that the Saudi born fugitive masterminded the devastating strikes on the U.S. According to the translation released with the tape Laden said "we calculated in advance the number of casualties from the enemy who would be killed based on the position of the tower. We calculated that the floors that would be hit would be three or four floors. I was the most optimistic of them all."

Laden's mother was quoted in a British paper on 23rd December as saying, she believed a video tape of her son, which the US said proves that Laden had prior knowledge of the September, 11 attack was fake. "I believe the evidence against him is not solid. I think the video they produced was doctored". "The voice is unclear and uneven, there are too many gaps and the statements are very unlike him" she said.

When the killers and those who were killed are no more on the scene, obliterating every piece of evidence by a horrific act of terrorism, how anybody could establish truth of the crime without confession by direct evidence.

6

MULLAH MOHAMMAD OMAR

Mullah Mohd.Omar was born in 1959 in the small village of Nodah near Kandhar to a poor peasants and lost his father when he was young and the responsibility of running the family fell on his young shoulders. He is the most secretive leader and not even a photograph of Mullah exists. He is believed to have been seen by two non-Muslims and indeed by few of his own 20 million Afghan people.

One story goes that in early 1994 Omar enlisted about 30 Talibans. Taliban means, "student of Islam". After hearing that, two teenage girls had been snatched from their village, by Mujahideen Commander and raped, he gathered the Talibans and with 16 rifles the group attacked the base and freed the girls. In the process he captured large quantities of arms and ammunition.

Another legend is that, as a junior commander fighting the Soviet forces he was hit on the eye by a sharpnel, while praying in his village mosque with blood oozing from the wound and realising that the eye was gone for good he pulled out of its socket with his own fingers .The fingers were then wiped on the mosque's wall. Visitors to Singesor are shown those bloody prints. Although anointed as Amir-Ul-Momineen (leader of the faithful) he is an illiterate from the point of Islamic theology.

He also retrieved the sacred cloak of the Prophet Mohammad from the Khandhar shrine where it had laid in darkness for sixty years and was cheered and applauded by delighted Mullahs assembled before him.

He has brought trouble for his movement and his Government. He defied the US, the United Nations and earlier hurt millions by ordering the destruction of the Bamiyan Buddhas.

Laden cultivated him by first buying over a mosque at Binnori, outside Karachi that Omar headed and then building a house for him. In addition, Laden gifted him a house in Kandhar's upmarket Shahr-I-Na (New Town) where he lives with three wives and five children.

Both Laden and Omar are cult figures wedded to a common cause of spreading and exporting their brand of Islam through means of fair or foul. They are also married the other's daughter and the one has given his daughter in marriage to the other's son. It looks very unusual but the truth is as elusive as the persons themselves. By comparison, Laden comes from a rich family and well educated and whereas Omar comes from a poor peasants family having humble beginning both as a fighter and cleric.

The puritanical Taliban under the leadership of Omar have introduced a strict interpretation of "Koran" as the basis for law and one of their edicts makes it mandatory for all men to grow beard at least as long as the width of a fist. The penalty for not doing so is intimidated. "Any one observed who has shaved and or cut his beard, are arrested and imprisoned until their beard gets bushy "said an edict issued in 1996 after Taliban seized the capital. To prevent the British and the US hair style, people with long hair were arrested and taken to the religious police to be shaved. The criminal has to pay to the barber.

Islam forbids the use of opium. According to the "Fatwa" issued by Omar, "though Islam prohibits use of opium it is not sin to grow and selling it to non-Muslims". The "Fatwa" appears to be funny and the drug production is continued without any hindrance though the United Nations came up with hefty funds for an anti-narcotics campaign.

The German Federal Police Bureau revealed that the hit list signed by Omar contain the name of the Afghan King Mohd. Zahir Shah, communists and members of the Northern Alliance.

Mullah Mohd.Omar and Mullah Akthar Mohammad Usmani were schoolmates. They both fought against the Soviet Russia. Both started together at the Jamia Farooq Azam Madrasa in Southern Kandahar province and after finishing the studies they worked as teachers together. Usmani is a man of simple tastes and takes only bread and fruit. Taliban leader Omar, therefore appointed him as his new deputy and eventual successor and reported to have gone into hiding for security reasons.

SEARCH FOR MULLAH MOHD. OMAR

After declaration of war by the US some of the senior Taliban members who defected to the Northern Alliance blamed Laden for transforming Afghanistan into a terrorist haven. Mullah Mohd Khaqzar former Taliban Deputy interior minister said Omar fell under the influence of Laden.

"Islam" Omar preached to his backward and destitute nation of twentyfour million people was the solution to all problems; poverty did not matter as long as Afghan souls were pure and they behaved in accordance with the stringent rules issued from Omar and his acolytes. Life, Omar decreed to be simplicity itself, an ascetic Islamic utopia. After bombing of his house by the US people actually came to know that Omar was not practising what he preached. The man who gave birth to Taliban government built himself his family and his Arab body guards just below an elephant mountain,a lavish palace of gaudy pink bathrooms, court yards, garages larger than most Afghan homes.

While the new Afghan government was working out for final details of deployment of thousands of international peace-keeping troops in Kabul the search for former Taliban leader Mullah Omar continued who went into hiding after the fall of Kandahar.

By the end of December the US and Afghan Anti-Taliban forces appeared to be zeroing in on Taliban spiritual leader Omar in the mountains of Southern Afghanistan. A fairly consistent body of intelligence suggested that Omar may be hiding near Baghran in Afghanistan's Southern Helmand province about 160 Km northwest of the Taliban's stronghold of Kandahar.

The first of more than one thousand troops from the US Army's 101st airborne division arrived in Southern Afghanistan city of Kandahar to assume duties performed by the US marines. The rotation came as an operation aimed at capturing Omar and to end the Taliban and Al-Qaeda leadership. There were confirmed reports that Omar was hiding somewhere in Baghran.

Some Anti-Taliban said that about twenty Non-Afghan fighters that trained with Al-Qaeda were among the estimated one thousand to fifteen hundred pro-Taliban forces that Pentagon authorities estimated were holding out in Northern Helmand. Omar, the Taliban Supreme leader might be among the holdouts.

Tribal elders and the US forces had thought Omar had taken refuge in mountainous Baghran, a northern corner of Southern Helmand province after he surrendered Kandahar at the first weekend of December. The Anti -Taliban forces said that" if Omar was here, if we knew he was here and we caputred him we would kill ourselves".

According to a report, Omar escaped on motor cycle as Anti-Taliban forces closed in on a mountainous area in Southern Afghanistan where he was believed hiding. Afghanistan's interim Prime Minister vowed that Omar will be arrested, though the government believes he probably eluded Anti-Taliban forces that reportedly had him surrounded and were negotiating his surrender.

While the senior members of the Taliban had surrendered including three Ministers, it is believed that Omar was probably still hiding in southern Afghan Province of Helmand. Baghran is a very big mountainous area and, therefore, it was difficult to find him quickly. Thousand of forces were looking for him.

Mullah Mohd Omar survived a direct US missile strike on his home and fled with his second wife in a Taxi. The fugitive's driver said it on the twenty first of January. He escaped a second pinpoint attack on the cab a little more than an hour later. "The missile struck and all of Omar's family ran outside in panic and Omar asked his driver to get a taxi."

Apprehensive of the American attacks, the Taliban Supreme leader whose words once were the law of land, placed the Afghans to leave in lurch and hiding in some unknown place.

7

REACTION OF WORLD LEADERS

The horrendous and horrible attacks on the World Trade Center and the Pentagon by the terrorists brought the whole world on the tenterhooks of world war. Several world leaders condemned the attacks as brutal and barbaric.

French President Jacques Chirac condemned the attacks as monstrous and expressed his solidarity with the American people. German Chancellor Gerhard Schroeder condemning the attacks said that "This day has changed the world. A terrible event, the scale of which we cannot yet appreciate". He told the *Frankfurter Allegemine Sonntagazeting* that he had information to support the allegation that Bin Laden was behind the attacks. The justified suspicions lead directly to Laden, his entourage and his helpers.

Tony Blair the British Prime Minister immediately summoned the security meeting and promised the British help to find the perpetrators. On the last day of September the British Prime Minister said that he had seen, "powerful and incontrovertible evidence" linking Laden to attacks in the US. He told the B.B.C Television, much of it came from intelligence services and other sensitive sources and the leaders were still figuring out how to present to the public". He also warned the Taliban ruling regime of Afghanistan saying that "they either help us or become the enemy themselves". He said that it was a war between the civilized world and fanatism.

Condemning the terrorist attacks on key cities of the US, Prime Minister Atal Behari Vajpayee of India said that time has come to redouble the global efforts to meet the challenges posed by terrorism and raise the voice against the menace to fight it out.

The immediate reaction of the Palestinian President Yasser Arafat was that "The attacks are completely shocking and unbelievable" and donated blood on the very next day of terror attacks for victims of the U.S. and observed a minute of silence in memory of the dead. The Democratic Front for the liberation of Palestine has denied that it carried out the attacks on the World Trade Center and the Pentagon. However thousands of Palestinians after terror attacks chanted, that "God is Great".

The U.S. foe Libya condemned the terror attacks and the Libyan leader, Muammar Gadhafi offered condolence of the horror of attacks. Iran President, Mohammad Khatami condemning the attack offered his deep sympathy to the American Nation.

President Vladimir Putin of Russia termed the attacks as "barbarous aimed against wholly innocent people, cause us anger and indignant and the entire International Community should unite in the struggle against terrorism". He assured that his country would provide weapons to the Anti-Taliban Northern Alliance and open Russian air space for humanitarian cargo.

President, Fidel Castro another enemy of the US warned of dangerous days ahead and urged the U.S. leaders to keep calm.Canadian Prime Minister, Jean Chrelien said that the terrorist attacks in the U.S. were "the equivalent of war".

Australia, which has over 100 nationals working at the World Trade Center, came out supporting the U.S. The Acting Australian Prime Minister, John Anderson expressing outrage at the onslaught on the cities of the U.S. said soon after that "the Australian Government will participate in whatever action" is needed internationally.

Japan, which has lost about 100 of its nationals working in the World Trade Center, promised full cooperation of the U.S. retaliation.

Sweden and Norway have admitted to a substantial presence of networks in Scandinavia with links to Bin Laden and Pakistan guerilla groups.

The China Government denied of having any close diplomatic and other ties with Afghanistan as they closed down its Embassy to Afghanistan in 1993. They, however, made it very clear that they are opposed to all norms of terrorism. They are of the view that no double standard should be maintained to fight against it.

Ireland feels close kinship to America and personal sense of loss as about 44 million Americans are having Irish ancestry. Prime Minister, Bertic Ahern condemning the attacks on the U.S. said that the Republic of Ireland came "as near as you can to close a country".

Prime Minister Helen Clark confirmed that New Zealand would join in international coalition to fight terrorism offering intelligence service and highly competent special force.

The Uzbekistan also expressed its support by lending military airbases to the U.S. forces for staging strikes against the terrorist targets in the neighboring Afghanistan.

Former Prime Minister Margaret Thatcher said that " who brought down those towers were Muslims, and Muslims must stand up and say that it is not the way of Islam. Passengers on those planes told that they were going to die and there were children on board. They must say it was disgraceful. I have not heard enough condemnation from Muslim priests."

Henry Kissinger, former U.S. Secretary reacting sharply at the attacks has said that the U.S. response to Tuesday terror attacks should produce results similar to the area produced by the American nuclear attack on Japan after Pearl Harbour

In the World War II Germany was defeated. The Japanese

backed by well established and intact industrial base were bent upon prolonging their war causing misery to the people of other nations under their control. They bombed Pearl Harbour on Oahu Island. Hawaii, the operating bases of the United States Pacific Fleet in 1941 resulted in the immediate entry of the U.S. into World War II and opened the pacific phase of the war.

In late 1941 more than 75 U.S. warships including battle - ships, cruisers destroyers, submarines and auxiliaries were based at this "Gibraltar of the pacific". All U.S. aircraft carriers were elsewhere. On November, 26 a Japanese task force consisisting of 6 carriers, 2 battle ships, 3 cruisers and several destroyers and tankers under the command of Vice Admiral Chuchi Nagumo departed in secret from the Kuril Islands. Observing radio silence it reached a launching point at 6.00 a.m. December, 7. At 7.50 a.m. the first wave of Japanese planes struck Pearl Harbour bombarding airfields and battle ships moored at the concrete guays. A second wave followed. The surprise attack was over before 10.00 a.m.

The results were devastating; 18 U.S. ships were hit and more than 200 aircrafts destroyed or damaged. The battle-ship *Arizona* was a total wreck. The *West Virginia* and *California* were sunk and the *Nevoda* was heavily damaged. Approximately 2,400 Americans were killed, 1300 wounded and 1000 missing. Japanese losses were fewer than 100 casualities, 29 planes and 5 midget submarines. The Japanese scored a brilliant tactical victory, apparently crippling the U.S. naval power in the pacific.

The attack was however a colossal political and psychological blunder, for it mobalised the U.S. public opinion against the Japanese and served as the catalyst that brought the US into the war. To curtail the war there was no other alternative save to decimate the Japanese's Industrial back bone. For that matter the Japanese themselves are guilty of compelling America to end its neutrality and enter into the war by unwarranted attack on Pearl Herbour of the USA in December, 1941.

Jordon King Abdullah met President Bush to seek to build

up a U.S. led coalition in the war on terrorism. The king was the first Arab Head of State to meet President Bush.

Besides Uzbekistan, Tejikistan has also accepted the U.S. request to allow Commander of Special Operation unit for launching strikes from their soil. So, also the former Soviet Republics which border the Northern Afghanistan.

NATO Secretary General, Lord Robertson said that the U.S. gave its NATO allies, "clear and compelling evidence that points conclusively to involvement of Laden and his Al-Qaeda network in the September 11 attack on New York and Washington. Mr. Robertson said, further the allies have determined that the attack was directed from abroad and, therefore, covered by NATO's article 5 which says that an attack on one member is an attack on all. He assured the U.S. that they can rely on the full support of its NATO Allies.

After its failure to convince the Tailban to surrender the fugitive Laden, the United Arab Emirates (U.A.E) snapped its ties with the Taliban on the 22nd September 2001. The U.A.E President Sheik Zayed Bin Sultan at Hayan spoke to President Bush and reaffirmed his opposition to terrorism in all its forms and manifestations saying that terrorism is repugnant to Islam and to other revealed religions.

President Mohammad Khatemi also reiterated for a global fight against terrorism but also for keeping peace. Saudi Arabia, which is considered the cradle of Islam snapped its ties with Kabul after two weeks of terrorists attacks and effectively undermined the legitimacy of its call for "Jehad". It said that the decision was because the Taliban Government did not pay attention to all the contacts and attempts by Saudi Arabia to persuade to stop harbouring the criminals and terrorists.

On 14th September with flags flying at half-mast, the United Nations Security Council condemned the attacks and called on the world to help find the perpetrators and those who sheltered them.

The Pope was extremely shaken by the attacks which he has called a dark day in the history of humanity. He urged the world not to allow spirit of hate and violence to prevail. The Pope went to his Private Chappal in the Pappal summer residence at Castelgandofo Rome. He retreated into silent prayer for the victims of the terrorist attacks that struck the U.S. on Tuesday the 11th September and to implore comfort for the injured and for reconciliation and peace in the world.

Even the United Nations Security Council has passed a resolution supporting the U.S. action against terrorism and those who harbour terrorists which had been supported by all the Islamic countries.

Undoubtedly such conventions and resolutions provide an umbrella under which countries wishing to co-operate may do so but it is far from being effective against those countries that regularly sponsor terrorism.

The Security Council decision asking the Taliban to hand over Bin Laden, "immediately and unconditionally to appropriate authority fulfils a condition many countries including Iran and China have been insisting for their approval of action that the U.S. has been contemplating against Afghanistan. It was also a face-saver for the Taliban in as much as they will not be seen bowing to the dictates of the lone super power.

While the icon of the world's greatest city was demolished, the Hurriyat Conference Chariman Abdul Ghani Bhat condemned terrorism in all its forms and at all levels anywhere in the world and, therefore, resolved to join the American people body and soul together to deal with terrorism in accordance within the principles of justice.

In a sign of their accelerating rapprochement in the wake of the attacks on the U.S. the Defence Minister of Russia and the NATO vowed to work closely together in the fight against global terrorism. Though the entire U.S. mourned the death of large number of people at the World Trade Center and the Pentagon, 90% of the population asked the U.S. Government to use military force to retaliate the attacks. President Bush, who is convinced of the world war against terrorism talked to all the international leaders on the telephone and has begun face to face campaign to win support for a global war against terrorism.To fight terrorism, President Bush has also asked Bangladesh support for over flight clearance, refulling facilities and use of airports, seaports for attack on Afghanistan.

In the wake of many countries supporting the U.S., Pakistan has also decided to back global efforts to combat terrorism and pulled out its diplomatic staff from Afghanistan for fear of war.

Former President Clinton heartily applauded President Bush's efforts to trace Bin Laden including the war he launched against the Taliban. Clinton himself battled Bin Laden in 1998 when his cruise missiles were fired at Laden's training camps in Afghanistan and a Sudanese factory that allegedly made a precursor to chemical weapons. In a display of wartime political unity the Republican and Democratic members of the U.S. Congress saluted President Bush's nationally broadcast call to arms. "Tonight we answer that call" replied Senate majority leader Tom Daschle." We are resolved to work together not as Democrats or Republicans but as Americans.

A U.S. poll taken after President Bush addressed Americans on 30th September found overwhelming support of 91 percent, the way President Bush was handling the U.S. response to the attacks. In Pakistan, however, the radical religious activists on 21st September violently protested against the possible U.S. strikes in Afghanistan. In a rare honour, New York city Mayor Rudolph Giuliani had the rare distinction of addressing the 189 member UN General Assembly on terrorism and to combat the scourge.

After a two day summit at Shanghai at the end of third week of October involving the U.S. President Bush, and his counterparts including China, Russia and Japan condemned the terrorist attacks in America as "murderous deeds" and demanded international co-operation in fighting terrorism.

The annual debate of the U.N General Assembly meeting at summit level was postponed in the wake of September 11 terrorist strikes in the U.S. from November 10th to 16th. This was the first time in the 56 years of the U.N that the high level segment of the annual session addressed by Heads of State and Government was postponed.

Mr. Ahmed Shah Masood, Commander-in-chief of the Anti-Taliban Northern Alliance was assasinated by the Taliban forces led by Bin Laden.

The assassination of Mr. Ahmed Shah-Masood, a vetran of the North Alliance, had a crippling blow in the organization. The Alliance military council named Mr. Fahim as his replacement. The Alliance was in contact with the U.S. officials and promised to co-operate in any U.S. strike of Afghanistan ruling Taliban.

When India was crying alone to condemn terrorist attacks on its soil, no big power of the World was able to appreciate and took notice of the menace. It should have been nipped in the bud itself instead of taking a neutral stand appeasing the aggressor. Taking advantage of the insouciant attitude of the super powers the terrorists have grown into leviathans and spread their tentacles as long as to strike America and issue threats to others. After the terrorists attacks on America now the World has felt the trauma what India was suffering from a long time and unamuinously called upon the nations to end terrorism in any part of the globe.

8

INVOLVEMENT OF BIN LADEN

In the interview to the Qatar based Arabic Channel *Al-Jazire*, which was recorded two years ago, Mr. Bin Laden has claimed Islamic rights over Pakistan nuclear bomb. "We supported the Pakistani people and congratulated them when God was gracious enough to enable them to acquire the nuclear weapon. We regard this as one of our rights and Muslims rights".

Bin Laden also said in the interview that he is actively looking to pile more nuclear weapons as well as chemical and biological weapons. It is the duty of the Muslims to posses them. His intended targets reportedly are the U.S. Britain and Israel". We believe that the right to self-defence is to be enjoyed by all people. Israel is stock piling hundreds of nuclear warheads and bombs and so also the Christians." He said that here are two parties to the conflict. The world Christianity, which is allied with Jesus and Zionism, led by the U.S. Britain and Israel. The other is the Islamic world. In such a conflict it is unacceptable to see the first party mount attacks, desecrate my land and holy shrines and plunder Muslim oil. When Muslims put up resistance against this party they are regarded as terrorists. This is stupidity. It is an insult to people's intelligence." "We believe it is our religious duty to resist this occupation with all the power we have and to punish it using the same means it is pursuing against us".

In this regard it is pertinent to note that Saudi Arabia withdrew the citizenship of Bin Laden in 1994 over his terrorist activities and criticism of the Royal Family. He is living in exile in Afghanistan and the Afghans treat him as a mere "guest".

The U.S. is exploring all over the world to trace out the man behind the 11th September attacks on New York City and Washington. It has reported that the 19 suspects in the air borne assaults on the U.S. spent 5,00,000 dollars preparing the operations and four of the hijackers were trained in camps in Afghanistan run by Bin Laden.The U.S. intelligence officials believe that the September 11 terror attacks were plotted in Germany. The official said that some of the hijackers held planning sessions in Hamburg and enrolled in flight training elsewhere in Europe. The FBI knew that 19 suspected hijackers had died on four planes and eleven more are part of the plot.

The Regional and Federal sources said that six people of Arab origin who were allegedly planning an attack on the British Embassy in Hamburg had been in contact with Mohammad Atta one of the hijackers identified in the attacks on the World Trade Center and the Pentagon. Pakistan, which has become a haven to the terrorists involved in the Egyptian hijacker Mohammad Atta receiving 1,00,000 dollars through a wire in the past year. The T.V channel further claimed that the wire transfer from Pakistan, were sent to Atta through two banks of Florida where Atta lived there much at that time.

The FBI has found evidence to link Sheik Omar who was released by India to meet the demand of hijackers of IC-814 plane at Kandahar to September 11 terrorist attacks on the World Trade Center which claimed thousands of lives. Sheik Omar was arrested by the Indian security force in 1994 and was lodged in Tihar Jail in India for years. Once he was released in Kandahar, Shaik Omar fled to Karachi. Captain Sharma of India Airlines Bus Air 300 which was hijacked to Kandhar on the eve of Christmas observed a number of striking similarities between the commandeering of his plane and the September 11 hijacking of the U.S. planes. He is not sure that they were the followers of Bin Laden but during the seven days of ordeal he found them as admirers of Bin Laden. He said that there was also similarity over the weapons used in both the hijacking episodes. The hijackers of his plane also used knives to hurt two passengers as in the case of hijacking of the U.S. planes.

In order to counter the argument, that Bin Laden has unnecessarily been involved in the terror attacks, the U.S. Secretary of State, Colin Powell after about a fortnight of the attacks stated that evidence of Saudi dissident Laden's involvement in the September 11 terror attacks will be presented "so that everybody will see the case cleanly as we do". He, however, stressed that the U.S. had to protect its sources and methods." Foreign Minister of Pakistan, Abdul Sattar revealed that the U.S. showed 20 pages of a document besides an oral presentation of Laden's involvement in the September 11 attacks and asked America to publicize it all over the world to enable people to make a fair judgement. Though he praised America for the good work done within a short span of time he was still in doubt to formulate a "fair judgement".

Strongly backing the U.S. in its war against terrorism the Indian leaders affirmed that Washington has not made any specific request for logistical support in the light of retaliating American strikes in Afghanistan. India which is plagued by the horrors of terrorists took advantage of the situation and their investigating agencies have handed over to the FBI crucial documents including video tapes, highlighting the diverse role being played by Taliban and Bin Laden trained militants in Pakistan and Jammu and Kashmir.

After the terrorist attacks in New York and Washington the experience of India of such nightmare of synchronized blasts in Mumbai eight years ago came to the light again. Dawood Ibrahim, a notorious criminal who master minded the ghastly blasts sneaked into Pakistan before the Indian Government could book him. The Interpol has issued "red corner" notices against him and he continues to reside in Karachi in full view of anybody who would care to look. Perhaps, President Musharraf do not care to see the criminal and therefore during the course of summit conference at Agra he told India without mincing any words that Dawood was not in Pakistan. There will not be any greater lie than this.

For the first time, Laden has admitted on 11th November that Al-Qaeda group carried out the attacks on the twin towers of the World Trade Center and the Pentagon on September, 11 and further threatened the lives of President Bush and British Prime Minister Tony Blair and warned Australia, Germany and Japan to stay out of the conflict. "The twin towers were legitimate targets, they were supporting the US, economic power" and the pilots who hijacked the planes were blessed by Allah" said Laden. He said further that "history should be a witness that we are terrorists. Yes we kill their innocents". In the video footage which was shot in the Afghan Mountains at the end of October, a smiling Laden goes on to say that the killing of atleast 2800 people was justified because they were" not civilians" but were working for the American system. The video which has been circulating for fourteen days among his supporters in the network formed as a centre piece of America's and Britain's new evidence against Bin Laden.

Before the Americans could make the above documents public Laden himself confessed the crime. Though President Bush convinced the World leaders of the involvement of Laden there was still a modicant of doubt in the Islamic Countries that the US and other western Europeon countries have declared war against Islam. From the self confession of Laden all the doubts must have been cleared in Islamic and other countries.

In the first interview after September 11 attacks to a Pakistani journalist Laden has once again justified the deaths of thousands of innocent people with his rabid rhetoric about Islam being under threat. He identified the reigning fears of the day by claiming he had amassed weapons of mass destruction. In the second, video said to have been taped in the end of October for private circulation among Al-Qaeda cadres he says" we will kill their innocents." He goes on to explain the reason for choosing the twin towers to make a dramatic of war no matter how many civilian causalities may have resulted.

Hamid Mir, official biographer of Bin Laden and editor of Urdu News Paper '*Ausof*' said that during the course of the interview Laden dropped broad hints of acquiring the nuclear capability from the Central Asian Republics "Laden referring to some reports appeared in the Western media said that some seventy nuclear weapons were stolen from Russia and these weapons are available in the underworld of the Central Asian States and anybody can purchase them.

The former Pakistan Premier Benazir Bhutto who was in New Delhi in the last week of November revealed that Laden's Al-Qaeda Network made two abortive attempts to assassinate her in 1993 and spent more than five million dollars to defeat her in the no confidence motion moved against her in early 1990s.

Though the fugitive terrorist, Bin Laden is believed to be hiding either in Afghanistan and Pakistan border or in Yemin he continues to issue threats on the immorality of the West via audio rather than video. The Al-Qaeda network which claimed responsibility for attacks on an Israeli airliner and suicide bombing at a hotel in Mombasa on 28th November 2002 that killed thirteen Kenyans and three Israelis confirm the fact that they were not only issuing threats now and then but also active in their clandestine operations and strike wherever and whenever possible.

9

DENIAL OF BIN LADEN

Anticipating the U.S. attack Bin Laden sneaked out of Afghan town of Kandahar to a safer place in the countryside with his four wives and several children. He denied that he had any hand in Tuesday's terror attacks in the U.S. Afghanistan ruling Taliban said that they felt responsible for the security of Laden. One of the leading papers of Pakistan reported that Laden took oath of allegiance from 500 of his Arab supporters in Kabul and shifted to an unknown place. Knowing the impending danger of military action by the U.S. in Afghanistan, the Taliban ruling party after about a week of the terror attacks said that Laden was missing. The claim was received with absolute disbelief by the U.S. and they increased the reward from five million dollars to twenty five million dollars for information leading to Laden's arrest.

Afghanistan ruling purist Taliban movement has announced a "Jehad" or holy war against the U.S. The Deputy Chairman of the council of Ministers Mullah Mohammad Hassan Akhond said it was unimaginable that the terror attacks against the World Trade Center and the Pentagon have been committed by the Taliban or by Laden. He accused all imperialists in the world, Jews and Christians and their supporters saying that they were intending to destroy the Islamic order "at the cost of blood under this pretext". The Afghanistan ruling Taliban militia also denied the involvement of Bin Laden and asserted that they do not have any such installations, which is worth the price of one cruise missile. In a statement issued soon after the terror attacks, Laden said that no organized group or outfit including his group were capable of doing such strikes and, therefore, denied his involvement in the tragedy.

The Taliban regime continued to keep the world in suspense over the fate of Laden and the Taliban supreme leader Mullah Mohammad Omar said that allegations against Laden by the United States were a pretext to wage a war against Islam and at the same time offered to talk with the U.S. Appealing to the U.S. to show patience Omar maintained that Laden was incapable of carrying out such strikes and has denied his involvement. The Taliban supreme leader Mullah Mohammad Omar accusing the U.S. committing "atrocities" against the Muslim world said that the sad event in America was the result of cruel policies and was meant to avenge their cruelty". He further added that "you must think of where attack took place and who was behind it, but Afghanistan is being made, the target and preparations are being made to attack Afghanistan. He reiterated that Laden was incapable of planning the sort of sophisticated suicide hijacking, which levelled World Trade Center and part of the Pentagon on September 11.

It is reported from London on 30th September that military operations led by the U.S. and British on bases controlled by Laden were expected to commence within 48 hours. Meanwhile, Afghanistan ruling Taliban reported on 30th September that Laden is under their protection and vowed not to hand him over until the U.S. provides evidence of his involvement in the September 11 terror attacks. The U.S. quickly rejected the Talibans conditional offer.

As the clouds of war looming large, crucial and intense diplomacy took place between Pakaistan and the Taliban regime in Afghanistan. Though the Laden issue was unresolved during the discussions the Taliban was hopeful of defusing the crisis with the U.S. They however, appeared to be gearing up for war its airspace and deploying Soviet-era Sued missiles and an estimated 10,000 troops along its border with Pakistan. They also took measures to hide Laden. Pakistan had given the Taliban seventy two-hour deadline to accede to the request for handing over Laden to the U.S. Efforts at finding solution to the tangle of handing over Laden was in confusion as the Taliban was apparently buying time. Having spent twenty-four hours the Pakistan negotiators stayed for another day in Afghanistan. Indications of the Ulemas who attended the council were on the lines that they would not agree to handing over Laden without concrete proof of his involvement in terrorism even if the whole Afghanistan is devastated. America after giving sufficient time to hand over Laden, thought no other alternative save to declare war on Afghanistan to ferret out Laden from his hiding place.

10

HUNT FOR BIN LADEN

The search for the world's most wanted man six foot five inches tall Laden was started by CIA in 1998 itself. They sent teams of the U.S. officers to Northern Afghanistan in an attempt to persuade the leader of the Anti-Taliban Afghanistan opposition to capture and perhaps kill Laden. The CIA clandestine deal with Ahmed Shah Masood, the then military leader of the most sensitive and highly classified elements of broader long-term campaign was continuing unsuccessfully through the end of the Clinton administration and into the Bush administration to destroy the network of Laden. After innumerable checks and counter-checks through satellite and human intelligence the American and allied forces in Afghanistan were convinced that Laden was hiding in Pamir mountain range.

According to the U.S. officials the administration of the President Bill Clinton has secretly spoken with the Sudanese Government on a plan to seize the Saudi born extremist, but it could not be fructified. Laden had been living in Sudan at that time after being expelled from Saudi Arabia. "Had we been able to roll up Laden then, there would not have been September 11 tragedy" they said.

A case of so near, yet so far. The U.S. could have had Laden in its pocket, if a little known deal with Pakistan had worked out. In the year 1999 operation the CIA secretly trained and equipped approximately sixty ISI commanders to enter Afghanistan for the purpose of capturing or killing Laden. It was arranged by the then Prime Minister Nawaz Sharif and his chief of intelligence with the Clinton Administration in return for a U.S. promise to lift sanctions on Pakistan and provide an economic aid package. The plan was aborted after Mr. Sharif's ouster by Mr. Musharraf and the latter refused to hear the U.S. To eliminate Laden was so intense in the U.S. circle that there was no week that went by when the issue was not seriously discussed by the National Security Council according to the former Defence Secretary William Cohen. The Former U.S. President, Bill Clinton has admitted that he ordered the capture and possible assassination of Laden who Washington believes master minded the September 11 terror strikes. Mr. Clinton told reporters in New York that he gave go ahead for the clandestine operation following the 1998 bombings of the U.S. Embassies in Nairobi and Dar-es-Saloom attacks for which Laden has since been indicted in the U.S. As a matter of fact, the U.S. Government offered a five million dollars reward for Laden in 1998 when he was charged with the offence of bombing the U.S. Embassies in East Africa.

Germany's most flamboyant Internet multi-millionaire, Mr. Kim Schmitz offered after two days of terror attacks up to ten million dollars leading to the arrest of Laden. Seized with the death and destruction caused by terrorist strikes the U.S. declared war against those responsible for thousands of causalities in New York and Washington. Invoking the rough justice of America frontier, President Bush declared on 16th September that the U.S. wants Laden, the suspected mastermind of the September 11 attacks brought to justice "dead or alive"

President Musharraf after discussing with key aides after the terror attacks issued a statement assuring President Bush, "we regard terrorism as an evil that threatens the world community—all countries must join hands in this common cause." The developments put the Pakistan President in an uncomfortable position between the U.S. and the Taliban. To that effect pressure began to mount on Pakistan to compel the Taliban to hand over Osama Bin Laden.

Bowing to the wishes of world opinion, Afghan clerics recommended on the 20th September that Laden would leave their country "whenever possible "but did not give out specifics and the ruling Taliban later acknowledged the nature of edict. Washington, which has begun deploying troops and equipments as part of Infinite Justice rejected the recommendation and demanded the world's most haunted man be turned over to responsible authorities. The White House officials said that "it does not meet America's requirement and this is about much more than one man being allowed to leave voluntarily, presumably, from one safe harbour to another safe harbour."

If Laden leaves Afghanistan the number of places he can go is limited. He was the "guest" of the Taliban militia in Afghanistan since 1996. Following the 1998 twin bombings of the U.S. embassies in East Africa, the Taliban reportedly made contact with the Chechen leaders about moving its "guest" to a new home somewhere within the rebel Russian republic. The decision of the Council of Islamic clerics of Afghanistan asking Laden to leave Afghanistan was not a gain step, Mr. Abdul Sattar, Foreign Minister of Pakistan told to the reporters. He said the Afghan tradition of protecting their "guest" was the reason behind the clerics turning down Pakistan request to hand over Laden.

Afghanistan ruling Taliban, however, said to have finally located Laden and officially delivered him the decision of the Islamic clerics council asking him to leave Afghanistan voluntarily in order to spare the country from the U.S. As the U.S. threatened military action in response to the September 11 attacks by hijacked airliners on New York and Washington that left more than 2800 people reported missing or dead, Pakistan had sent the clerics to persuade the ruling Taliban to hand over the Saudi born Bin Laden. Though the meeting of the Pakistan clerics and the spiritual leaders of Afghanistan and the ruling Taliban took place, the outcome of the meeting was discouraging as the ruling Taliban refused to extradite Bin Laden. The frustrated Musharaf has said that the Taliban days were numbered as they refused to the U.S. demand. He was not, however, prepared to break relations with Afghan militia.

The eighteen years old son of Bin Laden, Abdullah said that his father was hiding in a cave in the Afghan mountains with 300 commanders and would never be caught. Abdullah further said that his father disappeared with sixty trucks filled with satellite equipment and America and Britain will never track down him. He said, "I am not worried my father will be caught as he outsmarted the Americans for many years and Afghan earth will never give up my father".

The U.S. was maintaining round the clock vigil of the caves and tunnels in Afghanistan where Laden is suspected to be hiding. They said that the hunt for Laden narrowed to a few complexes of caves and tunnels. Inspite of the US led forces tightening the noose around Laden, reports have come out that Laden has been spotted in Kandahar. He was said to have been in the city to boost the morale of the people who have been braving carpet bombing unleashed by the US at the beginning of November. It was reliably learnt that Laden was hiding in one of the longest caves. In the second part of his interview with Hamid Mir, the editor of Urdu daily, Laden said that America would not be able to catch him alive". "I can be killed but my mission will not remain un-accomplished."

The Secretary of State Donald Rumsfeld suspected that Laden may try to out-manoeuver them by sneaking out of Afghanistan in a helicopter down one of those valleys that they could not pickup and pop over to some part of the country where there is an air field and have a plane waiting for Laden. However, the U.S. forces were trying to make it hard for Laden and flush him out of his hiding place.

An Arab News Paper reported that Laden had deployed ten look likes in Afghanistan to foil the US efforts at capturing him. It is also suspected that even if the American attacks against Afghanistan suceeded in finishing the Taliban movement they would not succeed in arresting Laden. Reports were also under circulation that out of the ten look likes of Laden two of them are North Africans and they were all in Afghanistan, only difference between them were birthmarks on their backs. Conflicting reports were reaching in the middle of November whether Laden was living in Afghanistan or left the place with his children and wives. In so far as the U.S. was concerned they had no information about his movements so also the Taliban Government.

Even after two months of battle and frantic search, the US could not locate Laden and Omar. The U.S. military was, therefore, broadcasting a radio message into Afghanistan on a reward of up to 25 million dollars for information leading to the location or capture of Laden. They were also of firm belief that Laden has not crossed the borders of Pakistan as the U.S. has provided more than one billion dollars to Pakistan, seventy three million dollars which was meant to increase the country's security along the border. *Al-Watan* newspaper reported that Laden has informed a number of people close and dedicated to him that he was living his last week or days and asked them to kill him before he is captured by the American troops. Some leading news paper agencies guessed that Laden might be based very close to Pakistan- Afghanistan border and Laden look alike would be killed to create a confusion and in the melee allow Laden to escape into Pakistan.

Leading news papers of the U.S. quoted that Laden has been spotted some where in the last week of November fifty six km Southwest of Jalalabad. He was also reported to have been seen near Tora Bora, a village where two valleys meet in deep mountains in Nangarhar province. Some people who have seen him said that "he was moving at night on horse back". At day he sleeps in caves.

As part of the Pakistan–U.S. co-operation in the war against terrorism and the US efforts to tighten its noose around Laden, the chief of the U.S. central intelligence agency George Tenet met President Musharaf and had detailed discussion with him in the beginning of the month of December. Despite the availability of latest equipment, the intelligence failure to track down the exact place of Laden had become a big perturbance for the U.S. The CIA has posted over a hundred commandos in Afghanistan to assist in the U.S. campaign to capture Laden and members of his Al-Qaeda Network and also sizeable number of personnel since September 11. The CIA was practically creating its own army, navy and airforce and has spent tens of millions of dollars on extra hardware.

Sahiba, one of the wives of Laden outlined the spectacular suicide plan saying that Laden planned to die on television to be projected as a "Martyr" before the U.S. led forces catch him hoping that his death would lead to a series of terror strikes on Capitol Hill in Washington, the Big Ben in London and Effel Tower in France. She said that "his elder sons will kill him and that will be signal for a new work of terror."

While the U.S. bombers sent of huge plumes of smoke along a mountain ridge near the eastern village of Tora Bora it was reliably learnt that Laden has eluded the U.S led forces seeking him in Afghanistan and fled to Pakistan with the help of friendly tribesmen. The same sources said that Laden's ninteen years old son Salahuddin remains at the groups base in Tora-Bora mountain cave complex.

In an interview on 25th December with the *Pakistan Observer*, one of the Taliban leaders said that the Al-Qaeda leader Laden was suffering from serious lung complications and succumbed to the disease for lack of adequate treatment. Laden was burried in his last abode and his grave was levelled as per his "Wahhabi belief" said the Taliban leader who claimed that he had attended the funeral. He also said that about thirty close associates of Laden including his trusted and personal guards and his family members attended the last rites. The Taliban leader who saw Laden's face before burial said that it seemed pale, but calm, relaxed and confident. On any feelings of remorse before his death the leader said , "No, instead, Laden was proud that he succeeded in his mission of igniting awareness in Muslims about the hegemonistic and conspiracies of "Pagans' against Islam. When asked about the place where Laden was buried he said, "I am sure that like other places in Tora-Bora, that particular place too must have vanished."

The U.S. intelligence who have not picked up any credible signs of Laden's where abouts suspected one of the three chief possibilities; Bin Laden was dead, killed by the U.S. bombs or his own followers. The new government in Afghanistan said that Laden has already slipped into Pakistan where he was being protected by the followers of radical Islamic leader Maulana Fazalur Rehman, a long time supporter of Laden and the Taliban. Top officials of the U.S. said, "we hear six, seven, eight conflicting reports every day about Laden location". "We have stopped chasing them". British Prime Minister, Tony Blair pledged to root out followers of militant Laden and provide support to Afghanistan new Government. After thorough investigation Pakistan Government came to know that two nuclear scientist got links with Laden. They therefore took steps to freeze the assets of Sultan Bashin-Uddin Mehmood and Abdul Majid who worked for Pakistan's Atomic energy commission. The State Bank of Pakistan also froze the accounts of wealthy industrialist Mohammed Tufail. All three were on the Board of Directors of *Ummah-Tameer-e-Nau* or Nation Builder, an Islamic charity and declared as a terrorists group by the United States on 20th of December.

The trial for the World's two most wanted men turned cold after Afghan officials said that the Taliban leader Omar had fled to a mountainous Southern area and Laden was on the run. As the U.S. rounded up more detainees in Afghanistan, the Pentagon sent a large number of troops to build and guard a high security detention facility at the U.S. navy base in Guantanamo Bay, Cuba that would hold as many as two thousand Taliban and Al-Qaeda prisoners. Several U.S. officials meanwhile pointed again to Pakistan as the most likely refuge for top fugitives Laden and Omar, as an intensified man-hunt for Omar in South Central Afghanistan has failed to turn up the chief of Afghanistan's defunct Taliban regime.

Frustrated so far in the manhunt for Laden and other top Al-Qaeda and Taliban leaders the U.S. commanders were shifting attention and troops from mountainous Tora Bora region in eastern Afghanistan farther South along the Pakistan border. American troops conducting interdiction missions in a rugged area near the eastern town of Khost apprehended fourteen armed Al-Qaeda fighters and took possession of lap tops, cell phones and training manuals carried by the group which could provide further intelligence about Al-Qaeda and Taliban resistance that continued in Afghanistan. The U.S. authorities were also pursuing one man as intensely as Laden himself an elusive Palestinian who they believed had been entrusted with keeping the terrorist organization's global network of cells alive and operational. As the U.S. forces searched for additional Al-Qaeda targets the U.S. intelligence still had no clear picture as to the whereabouts of Laden. They suspected that he was still in the Afghanistan-Pakistan border area. . The Pentagon down playing the importance of capturing or killing Laden and Omar expressed their most important task was to prevent further terrorist attacks on the U.S. and their allies.

Pakistan President Musharaff said Laden "is most likely dead because he has not been able to get treatment for his kidney disease. I think now frankly he is dead" said Musharaff. President Musharaff said in an interview published in Islamabad on eighteenth January that Laden might have died of kidney failure in a cave in Afghanistan after separated from a dialysis machine he has used in recent years.

Afghan Foreign Minister Abdullah Abdullah said in the last week of January that Laden was probably alive-possibly in Pakistan. "I have no reason to believe that he is dead" in response to questions on statements by President Musharaff that Laden has probably died of kidney failure.

The U.S. officials who expressed confidence that they had covered Laden in the mountain of Tora Bora acknowledged later in the first week of February that they have lost track of the terrorist leader and increasingly frustrated over the virtual absence of intelligence about his whereabouts. A pilotless spy plane joined the hunt for Laden. Across between a flying saucer and a helicopter, the disc shaped Simicaon Rotor Craft (SRC) looked like something out of cult space series. The American central intelligence agency was frantically hunting for an Afghan woman teacher who taught

English to daughters of Laden. Alam Bibi who is in her thirties was reported to be alive and hiding in the rugged mountains along Pakistan-Afghanistan border. Alam Bibi's family returned to Afghanistan after the Moscow-backed Government of Najibullah lost power in 1992 and at this place Laden moved along with his two wives, nearly a dozen children and hundred of Arab fighters. Bibi made friends with some of the educated.

The U.S. aircraft have launched bombing raids over parts of eastern Afghanistan near Pakistan border where remanants of the Taliban and Laden's Al-Qaeda were believed to be hiding. The U.S. aircraft bombed the Mafazatoo area of Gorboz district on the fifth and sixth of February and the bombing was very heavy. The U.S. officials in Washington said that a missile fired by remote control from a pilotless CIA aircraft had hit what was believed to be a group of senior Al-Qaeda members in the same general region, killing atleast one of them. It was not clear who the individual was as the bad weather in the region had prevented a mission to identify the body.

The Bush Administration has concluded that Laden was at Tora Bora when the US aircraft began bombing on 30th November,2001 but escaped because the American ground troops were not sent to pursue Al-Qaeda Leader. Intelligence officials have what they consider to be decisive evidence gleaned from interrogations and intercepted communication that Laden was inside Tora-Bora complex along Afghanistan's mountainous eastern border when the battle began but escaped during the first 10 days of December. Laden and one of his top lieutenants have reportedly spotted in Pakistan's semi-autonomous tribal belt. The reports suggested that Laden and Zawahiri might be in the village of Maidan in North Waziristan.

To the great embarrassment of Washington and to the disappointment of others World over neither Laden nor Taliban's Supreme Leader Omar have been captured even after thirty months of frantic search. The World's most hunted man has a $ 25 million reward on his head for allegedly masterminding the attacks on the

World Trade Center and the Pentagon. Laden's current where abouts are not known but it is presumed that he has dramatically shifted over the past few months from Afghanistan and Pakistan's border area to the law-less tribal region of Hadhra Mang in South east Yemen where his father was born. The suspected terrorist is regularly meeting Omar according to a telephone call intercepted by the American Satellites. The two men using a mobile Thurunga Satellite phone spoke about tactics for several minutes according to voice analysis reported by the "*Observer*" weekly. The U.S. officials presume that they were alive until presented with evidence to the contrary.

11

THREAT OF THE TALIBAN

In the wake of many countries supporting the U.S. and the U.S. declaring war against terror, Taliban Supreme Leader Mullah Mohammad Omar called on Muslims all over the World to face the threat of the U.S. attack firmly and prepare for "Jehad" to defend their faith. Afghanistan, which even cannot feed its people, has threatened retaliation if the U.S. attacked it. Laden has also warned the U.S. will be punished. The Taliban in a sterned tone asked the U.S. to withdraw its troops from the Gulf region and said 300,000 Afghan "experienced in Jehad" have been deployed in Kabul along the borders and other important sites. In its defiant mood, the Taliban took over the U.N offices in the Southern city of Kandhar and clamped a communication blackout on the world body's other operations and threatened to execute any U.N workers using key equipment in their offices in Afghanistan and scalded satellite telephone walkie, talkies and computers etc.

In a signed statement provided to Qatars, *Al Jazeera* satellite channel Laden exhorted the Pakistan's Muslims to fight the American forces and said that he was praying to God that they would be accepted as Martyrs. There were 1000 military advisers and 5000 Pakistanis who are products of "Jehadi Madrasses" in Afghanistan. India has information about 79 training camps run for Kashmir militants, in Pakistan and 126 more in Pakistan Occupied Kashmir. Mr. AL Chaidar, a Muslim activist told the daily, "*Rakyat Merdeka*" that a representative of Laden had made at least four visits to Indonesia the most populous Muslim country. Laden must have gone there to muster support of Muslims for his mission. The U.S. intelligence has uncovered information that Saudi exile Laden and his group Al Qaeda, acquired components for weapons of mass destruction from the Russian Mafia. In response to the threat of the U.S. one of the Pakistan's biggest Pro-Taliban religious parties has threatened to shoot down aircraft of the U.S. lead coalition forces if they launch attacks on Afghanistan from Pakistan. The Taliban forces in Afghanistan reported to have up to 100 shoulder fired stingers, the U.S. made missiles with deadliest record against low flying aircraft ironically supplied by the U.S. to the Afghan in 1980. However, from military point of view the stingers could not pose a major threat to the U.S. helicopters if Washington struck, Taliban bases in Afghanistan. The U.S. special forces and their helicopters usually operate under cover of darkness but stingers can be aimed easily only in daylight.

With strikes against Afghanistan became increasingly certain, the Taliban regime renewed its call to hold negotiations with the U.S. but remained non-committal on handing over Laden. The threat of the Taliban Supreme leader Omar to the mighty American was like a rat rattling to a ravenous lion to bring its own disaster.

12

OPERATION ENDURING FREEDOM

Operation Enduring Freedom is the U.S. code name for its military build-up in response to the September 11 attack. The first of 21st century and the new millennium has begun according to the President of America, as a war against the faceless and nomadic international terrorist in retaliation to the attack on America, which has been both frontal and visible. The damage caused to the world's strongest power, militarily, politically, and economically was incalculable. The U.S. was never so directly hit and the most Americans raised in comfort and affluence, ever saw war and destruction in their own country. The whole American nation is up in arms. In political circles it was being discussed that a war between the U.S. and Afghanistan will be a war between the world's most unequal powers, between the world's richest country and the world's poorest country. The imbalance between the two sides is so great as to make the fight look farcical.

The U.S. House of Representatives approved with a majority of 398-17 votes 344 billion dollars defence spending bill that shifts some missile defence funds into anti-terrorism programmes after the suicide hijacked attacks. In an effort to move closer to Afghanistan the U.S. war planes landed in the former Soviet Republic of Uzbekistan and President Vladimir Putin voiced readiness to co-operate with the U.S. plans to strike Afghanistan. The U.S. has identified certain airports in Pakistan from where it could possibly carryout assaults on Afghanistan or airdrop, food and medical supplies in the war ravaged country. Some of the places identified for air troop movements include Pasni, Gwadar and Quetta. It was first, however believed Washington might shelve plans for bombing raids on Afghanistan because of a shortage of viable targets, opting instead to deploy special forces. The U.S. and Pakistani delegations also discussed, "how to minimally use the ground force in view of the difficult topography of Afghanistan where mountains and deserts pose a major threat to the invading forces.

In a further move for preparation of war the U.S. aircraft carrier "*Kitty Hawk*" steamed out of its home port near Tokyo on the 1st of October on a mission to support the U.S. military response to September 11 attack on the World Trade Center and the Pentagon. The U.S. *Kitty Hawk* departed Yokosuka to support the tasks as assigned by the National Command Authority in response to the "Operations Enduring Freedom". The 81,123 - tones aircraft carrier escorted by several Japanese destroyers, left the Yokosuka base a day after returning to the port on exercise that lasted nine days. It is reported that Pakistan and its intelligence service have valuable information about what is occurring inside Afghanistan. But a former U.S. official said that joint operations with Pakistan service were always dicey, because the Taliban Militia that rules most of Afghanistan has penetrated the Pakistan intelligence. "You never know who you were dealing with. You are always dealing with shadows" said the former senior official.

The Americans had delivered to Russians latest models of anti-terrorist equipment hastily and the Russian troops joined their American counter-parts after a week of familiarization with these weapons. The Russian troops, which were inching towards Pamir, were fluent in *Pushto* language, while many have working knowledge of *Dari*. It is believed in Pakistan circles that the American and Russian forces have launched joint operations to track down terrorist Bin Laden in Pamir Mountain ranges. The British forces were also planning to launch anti-Taliban operations from the southern Afghanistan. "To reach Laden suspected hide-outs, advance parties of the U.S. commandos had already begun crawling from a launching site in Tajikistan since 4th of October. Russians had pointed at the suspected hide outs and provided route maps to some sites which were used for sorting the nuclear tipped missiles by the former U.S.S.R. during the culminating years of the cold war at the heights of Pamir.

While the U.S., Russian and British were planning to launch attack on Afghanistan, the Afghanistan Northern Alliance said on the 5th of October, that it was not going to wait for the U.S. strikes against the Taliban and would launch a major offensive against the militia by the evening of 6th October. As the clouds of war still looming large in Afghanistan, President Bush on the eleventh of January signed a 318 billion dollars defence spending bill. He described it as a "down payment" on expenses tied to the U.S. led war on terrorism. "Our military must have every resources, every tool, every weapon and every advantage" he said. Though it appears that a lion is trying to prove its might to a rat, President Bush, bereft of the above facts acted with circumspection and taken all diplomatic and military measures to force out the Talibans from Afghanistan and capture Bin Laden and Omar as early as possible.

13

FREEZING OF BANK ACCOUNTS

It is believed that a Sudanese Bank might have given Bin Laden access to banks in many other countries including the U.S. The bank created by Laden aide in 1991 with 50 million dollars as seed money from the militant leader who had access to the U.S. banking system through correspondent accounts services provided it to by the U.S. banks. "That means any customer of the Shamal Bank including a member of Bin Laden organizations could penetrate the U.S. banking system by going through one of these other correspondent accounts". Laden is thought to have several hundred million dollars rippling silently invisibly through bank accounts around the world.

Striking on the financial foundation of the terrorists, President Bush ordered freezing of the U.S. assets of Laden and 27 other outfits including Pakistan based, the *Harkat-Ul-Mujahideen* and has redesignated 26 groups including Osmana-Bin-Laden's groups as foreign terrorist organizations. Under 1996 Law, the U.S. citizens are prohibited from providing such organizations with assistance. Banks and other financial institutions must freeze their assets.A U.S. initiative to dry up the terrorist funds has led to the world-wide freezing of more than 24 million dollars in assets belonging to the Taliban and Al-Qaeda network. As a part of counter terrorist attack, the U.S. seized assets of ten other terrorist organizations. In order to cripple the flow of money for subversive acts by Laden, Pakistan's Central Bank has ordered Banks to freeze accounts held by the *Harkat-Ul-Mujahideen*, a militant group operating in Kashmir that was included on the U.S. terrorism black list.

Britain has also frozen 88 million dollars of financial assets linked to the Taliban, which was accused of harbouring Laden. Chancellor of the Exchequer, Gordon Brown of Britain stressed the importance of cutting off the flow of finance to terrorist and outlined new measures to strengthen Britain's anti-terrorist legislation particularly on the financial front.

To the rejoicement of India, the U.S and U.K banned Pakistan based militant outfit. *Jaish-e-Mohammad* (Jem) and froze its assets on 12th October. The above organization first claimed responsibility for the 1st October attack, on Jammu and Kashmir. The above two countries have also frozen the assets of another Pakistan based organization, the *Rabita Trust of Lahore*. It is unfortunate that the Indian Government requested the other countries like U.K. and the U.S.A. to ban various militant out-fits and seize their assets oblivious to the fact that they do not have any law to freeze or seize the assets of militants who have become menace to their country.

Laden, the world's most wanted man, controls a financial empire whose destruction was essential if the war against terrorism has to be carried to victory. It is the Saudi-born multi-millionaire himself who manages the funds belonging to "international terrorism". Britain continued its crack down on terrorist funding giving financial institutions a wide ranging new list of alleged terrorists organizations whose assets it wants to frozen. The treasury which has released two lists which contained the groups connected to Laden and his Al- Qaeda network and for individuals in Britain when the British thought to have ties with the Al-Qaeda. The new list of 25 groups includes *Babbar Khalsa,* a sikh group, *International Sikh youth Federation*, Pakistan based militant outfit, *Lashkar-e-Tayabba, LTTE* and the Japanese cult *Aum Shinri Kyo*. In order to appease the U.S.

the Pakistan Government has frozen the bank accounts of Kashmiri militant outfit, *Jaish-e-Mohammed*.

A rare gem from Tanzania hugely popular in the U.S. with a market price of 380 million dollars is a major source of income for Laden's Al-Qaeda network. Tanzanite had become a U.S. marketing phenomenon promoted by prestigious jewl stores as the most important gemological discovery in 2000 years. Tanzanite is so rare it is mined in only one place on earth- a five square mile patch of graphite rock in the Northeastern Tanzania.

The United Nations has ordered its 189 members to freeze assets of one hundred and fifty two Taliban officials, virtually everyone who held a Government post on behalf of former rulers of Afghanistan. The United Nations Security Council sanctions committee added another one hundred and twenty seven names of individuals, groups or business firms associated with the Taliban or Laden and his Al-Qaeda network.

14

FLEEING OF AFGHANS

Frightened with the U.S. attack thousands of Afghans left Afghanistan ignoring the Taliban's calls to stay and wage a "Jehad". The staff of the International Committee of the Red Cross also pulled out of Afghanistan. After the heat and dust restraint seemed to be the buzzword among the U.S. lead anti-Taliban coalition. After a fortnight of terror attacks, the Taliban supreme leader Mr. Omar said he saw less likelihood of the U.S. attack, since Washington had no proof that Laden was involved. He, therefore, appealed to the thousands of Afghans fleeing towards the border to return home.

Following through, on a threat to punish the ruling Taliban for not handing over Laden 1.5 million Afghan refugees left their country ahead of an unexpected U.S. attack. President Bush, therefore, earmarked 25 million dollars to meet the needs of the above refugees.

International terrorism is a grave menace to human security and international peace. Nuclear and biological weapons are now available to the terrorists and narco-terrorism is another modern menace sustained by money and drug smuggling. Religious fundamentalism has added fuel to the fire. Poor Afghans; It was Russia that invaded it and imposed many types of hardships on the people. Then came the Taliban, which made things worse for them. Their plight had been, movingly portrayed by Mohsen Makhamalabaf, Director of the movie, *Khandhar*. He depicted that the statue of Buddha (Bamiyan) was not demolished by anyone. It fell down out of shame. Out of shame for the world's ignorance of Afghanistan.

Sensing the dangers of death for want of food and clothing the United Nations Secretary-General Kofi Annan appealed on the 27th September, for 584 million dollars in fresh emergency aid for the Afghans facing what the United Nations is calling the world's worst humanitarian crisis. He said that Afghanistan population is about 26 million. After decades of war and three years of severe drought in the Central Asian nations some 5 million Afghans were already dependent on outside aid for their survival. The situation took a serious turn for the worst after the September 11 hijack attacks as the U.S. putting as many as 2 million more Afghans at risk. Responding to the appeal by the U.N. agency top Hollywood actress Angelina Jolie was the first person to donate a whopping one million dollars for Afghans. Tibetan spiritual leader the Dàlai Lama has donated fifty thousand dollars to help Afghans who have fled their country. India pledged one hundred million credit line to the next Government in Kabul as part of its policy to send in huge humanitarian and development largesse to the war-torn country. Taiwan has donated seven million dollars aid to Afghan refugees, the aid includes food, medicines, tents, blankets and clothing. They were donated by the Taiwan government, the Tzuchi Buddhist Foundation and other civic groups.

The United Nation has set up a fund to get the Government machinery in Afghanistan in motion and expects to raise at least 20 million dollars immediately. Money from the Afghan interim authority fund would be channelled towards building infrastructure and administrative expenditure for the interim government to start functioning.

15

TERRORISM AND JEHAD

In his book, *principles of Islam* Maulana Wahiduddin Khan writes, "Islam is a religion which teaches non-violence. According to the Koran God does not love violence. One is a good Muslim - and that is quintessential message – without wielding a gun and striking at the enemy targets."

Legally terrorism is defined as the sustained and clandestine use of murder, bombings and hostage taking to achieve a political purpose. Terrorism is more monstrous and reprehensible than war because it targets innocent civilians much more than war does. Terrorism is not a modern invention. Instinctive terrorism existed throughout the history and State Terrorism is as old as State itself. Most of the States today practice, "reign of terror" secretly to liquidate all of those opposed to the establishment. In the seventies of last century the rise of international terrorism was characterized by hijacking of planes and attack on diplomats.

Walter Lacquer the authority on terrorism and a prolific writer on the subject said that there are as many as one hundred and nine definitions of terrorism. The aim of the terrorist, wrote Lacquer, is to induce a state of fear in the victim. The terrorist is ruthless and does not conform to humanitarian norms. A Chinese Philosopher explained the terrorist tactic, "Kill one, frighten ten thousand". An IRA terrorist issued frightening warning to the then British Prime Minister, "you need to escape a thousand times a day, I need to succeed only once". Such a single act brought a tragic end to the lives of Indira Gandhi and her son Rajiv Gandhi in the last century.

Terrorism, caused by groups both national and international, has become a great menace and threat to human rights as terrorism is not selective but purposefully strikes the innocents taking out their lives.

Terrorism broadly falls into three categories.

1. Terrorism going by the name of "freedom struggle" without outside interference. Palestinians cause for their homeland falls under this category.
2. Terrorism sponsored from across the border by foreign nation like Pakistan in Jammu and Kashmir is the best example of cross-border terrorism.
3. State terrorism a military response by the nations affected by terrorism of the first and second category.

It is quite unfortunate that the U.N General Assembly failed to adopt even after a five day debate in the month of October 2001, a resolution over definition of terrorism and distinction between the scourge and the freedom struggle. Therefore in many countries where the terrorism has become a menace, it is feared that if with the U.N. we might fail then, without the U.N. we are bound to fail.

In view of the above Jehad (freedom struggle) in Kashmir is being fought stupidly in the name of so called Jehad which do not fall in any one of the three interpretations. To be more specific Kashmir is not an occupied land and as a matter of fact it is a part of the cultural, civilizational and political unity of India for over the centuries. There is neither religious intolerance nor social oppression. The Kashmir Muslims are not discriminated in law or in its practice and as a matter of fact since independence the State is ruled by Chief Ministers who belonged to the Muslim community. Since because majority of the population in the State consists of Muslims, it does not acquire the right to break from India.

In an effort to increase the number of militants, the Pakistan regime is brain-washing young Muslims under the guise of *Koran* teaching to produce an unlimited supply of male Jehads. Apart from the above, the Pakistanis were having more than one hundred schools in their country which were engaged in brain-washing girls as young as five to women as old as sixty five to "attain martyrdom" by fighting in Kashmir and elsewhere.

Black Tuesday has served notice that America is also not safe either at home or abroad exclusively on fire power or economic clout, but also on a global commitment to end poverty, destitution and injustice of every kind. Ordinary people all over the world have to seriously take note of that terrorism in the U.S. cannot be stopped as long as it is allowed in Kashmir.

Like most of other nations, the U.S. treated attack on their embassies in Kenya and Tanzania as an internal matter. After the terror attacks on the World Trade Center, the Pentagon and other places, the U.S. realized that threat of terrorism knows no borders. Citizens of eighty nations were known to have lost in September 11 attacks. Terrorists have killed innocent people and there is a rising tide of fear in the world that there is no public safety and property. It appears that the very foundations of civilized society had been shaken. The U.S. has, therefore acknowledged after a long time, the fact that the terrorists do not simply desire to kill individual Americans and innocent people in Jammu and Kashmir, but the democratic societies like those in India, the U.S. and elsewhere in the world. President Bush, therefore exhorted democracies to unite in this war against terrorism and prevailed upon his allies like the NATO, the United Nations, Russia, China and other Arab countries to support in the war of terror.

All the countries in the world, without any reservation should support America, without verifying the fact, as what moral right it has got to lead the compaign against terrorism while sitting itself on the stockpiles of weapons of mass destruction.

It is a fact that terrorism endangers all countries but the answer to this menace is not to nurture a monster like Bin Laden, the Taliban in Afghanistan and other militant groups in Pakistan but to evolve a counter, ideology to weaken the very forces that give rise to extremism. There are millions of Muslims all over the world who do not subscribe to wage, Jehad against all and sundry. It is the responsibility of these Muslims and their leading lights to come forward and openly condemn the acts of the terrorists who are causing colossal human tragedy in the name of Jehad.

Terrorism knows no boundaries, geographical, religious political and ethnic. Though there has been a rise in Islamic militancy in the last one decade, it is not correct to label Islam alone with terrorism. The IRA, LTTE, ETA are not Islamic groups.

Pakistan and the Taliban are epicenters of terrorism, providing training, inspiration and equipment. Saudi Arabia Iran, Iraq and Syria have been the paymasters. The U.S. and the Western Europe cannot claim the moral high ground and fight against terrorism. The banking and financial institutions of these countries were hosts to the terrorist money. One trillion U.S. dollars flow into European banks each year. Terrorists believed that their bigoted ends can justify the most diabolical means of terror of killing thousands of innocent people. They took the name of God and religion and called their campaign a Holy war only to excite sentiments and emotions and in a bid to mobilize wide support to their inhuman cause.

There are around seven thousand religious schools in Pakistan run with the financial contributions from sympathizers at home and abroad to spread religious militancy. More than half a million children and adults live and study in religious schools, thousands of them Afghans and hundreds from the Arab countries. Pakistani volunteers from various seminaries have fought in Afghanistan alongside the hard-line Taliban militia which appeared very dangerous. Pakistan Government is now moving to regulate these religious schools with avowed policy introduced teaching of modern subjects side by side with religious education in order to bring them into the main stream of the national educational system.

Jehad is a best moral doctrine representing civilizational urges of people to order their lives in the light of the Koran teachings. This is evidence by such a verse as, "he who exerts himself exerts only for his own soul which expressed the "Jehad"in terms of the salvation of the soul rather than a struggle for proselylitisations. Surely the meanings of Jehad have changed over the centuries and hot headed individuals and groups attempt to target innocent civilians.

With an evil design of establishing an Islamic State in the World in Afghanistan the Taliban chief Mullah Omar and the terrorist mastermind Bin Landen imposed diabolical cult on Muslims in the name of Jehad and Islam. What kind of "Islamic rule" the Jehadis wish to impose is well disclosed by an Afghan refugee. According to him the Muslim women are not allowed to move out of their houses without *Burqa* and they were not even permitted to get treated by male doctors. As education was prohibited to women, female doctors were rare. The innocent Muslim children were brainwashed thoroughly in *Madrasas* (clergy schools) to hate the non-believers of Islam. The moral police was so brutal in enforcing the "Islamic Law" that they shoot down the violators in public and cut off the hands of women not covered with, *Burqa*. Without any reservation and hesitation old men are allowed to marry minor girls. As a matter of fact women were treated as sex objects satisfying the carnal passion of their men.

Professor Karen Armstrong, the author of several books on Islam explains in her article, The *True and Peaceful Face of Islam* that the authentic import of "Jehad is the struggle against the infidel", in one's own self and society implying self conquest. Conquering the egoistic, dissolute and deceitful Satanic mind is the real implication of Jehad which, in fact, is the exhortation and precept of every other religion. She further quotes from the Koran that there must be no coercion in matters of faith and Muslims are enjoined upon to respect other religious people who worship the same God. Contrary to the above the Taliban (students of Islam) in the name of Jehad were indulging in hatred of other religions, violence and killing of innocents.

Jehad, in the first place, means a holy war against internal enemies within an individual as such as the lust for power, prejudice, pride, jealousy, miserliness, spreading scandal and violence which can be described as the seven deadly sins. The second interpretation of Jehad is war against oppression, political and economic prevailing in Muslim societies across the Arab world and Afghanistan where people's aspiration of civil and political rights and democratic governance is denied. War against oppression of Muslims by non-Muslims across the world comes under their interpretation of Jehad. In Islam-early days-Jehad was the war cry in the tribal-ridden society. Later, rulers employed the emotive slogan to justify military expansion. Today Jehad is the weapon of the strong military dictators and monarchs.

AMERICAN STAND ON TERRORISM

Attack on the Arab – Americans and Sikhs

The gruesome killing of thousands of innocent people in the World Trade Center aroused the feeling of vengeance in the U.S. Assuming Sikh as Arabs, Shri Balbir Singh Sodhi was killed in Mesa (Arizona) and fifty to sixty Sikhs were attacked. The race hate against the Muslims simmered in Australia and a mosque was set on fire and bombed there.

While Pakistan was alerting its troops on Pakistan border, the Saudi Crown Prince, Abdullah, offered help to the U.S. to find out the perpetrators of attacks and cautioned against blaming the Arabs and Muslims in general for the attacks on countless Arab-Americans who have received death threats and anti-Muslim messages since Black Tuesday attacks. As the days were passing, President Bush got a powerful political boost and the nation rallied with demand for swift retaliation. In the wake of terrorist strikes, attacks were made on about 50 to 60 Sikhs of the U.S. often mistaken for Arabs. Therefore, President Bush urged the Americans not to take vengeance against the Arab-Americans.

In order to counter the surge of sentiments against Muslims, Sikhs and other minorities, President Bush after assuring their leaders condemned the assaults on minorities and said that, "they do not represent the best of America, they represent the worst of human kind, and they should be ashamed of that kind of behavior."

Black Tuesday has been a tragedy in two senses, first in terms of loss of thousands of innocent human lives and resources, second in terms of long term damage to the American way of life.

Consequent of terror attacks, a pulp patriotism raised its ugly head, and all Asian minorities have become targets of such vandalism and racist attacks.

American move to punish its terrorists are running into severe criticism in several countries though they extended their support against the terrorist attacks in New York City and Washington. India, of course, lost two Prime Minister to terrorists attacks and has been continuously losing uniformed men and innocent civilians in Kashmir. Mindless terrorists have been kidnapping and killing tourists in the Philippines for many years. Sri Lanka and Palestinians are no exception. Terrorism as a political weapon became potent in the hands of Pakistan and Israel and the U.S. supported these States. This record of double standards is what is eating into the America's creditability when it calls for world alliance against terrorism.

Expressing disapprobation of the attacks some of the leading papers in India came heavily on the U.S. Government reminding them of the fact that despite conclusive of moral, material and logistic support, terrorism in Jammu and Kashmir has been receiving from across the border of India. The U.S. has been extremely reluctant to respond to India's charge. As a consequence of such reluctance, terrorism assumed monstrous proportions in the sub-continent equating terrorism with a Jehad.

Notwithstanding this double standards of the U.S. the Prime Minister of India declared every Indian has to be part of this global war against terrorism and the entire Nation observed two minutes silence as the clock struck 10.30 am on the 18th of September.

There is a feeling in India that neither the Bombay blasts nor the fact that Pakistan is harbouring the prime suspect in those blasts, Dawood Ibrahim, nor the hijack of the Indian Passenger Plane to Kandhahar in Afghanistan on the millennium eve stirred the American Government and their media at all. It has paid mere lip sympathy for combating terrorism across the world looking over its shoulder clearly unconcerned when it came to other affected parties. As matter of fact, two years ago, Indian intelligence had alerted the Americans when the trial of a top Kashmir terrorist killed in an attack by the BSF led to the South East School of Aeronautics, Georgia where he had obtained 700 hours of flying experience before working for an outfit controlled by Bin Laden.

Though India condemned the cowardly and horrific act of hijackers in blowing out the World Trade Center and part of the Pentagon, they are still not forgetting the fact of the double standards of America. As a matter of fact Bin Laden is a creation of the U.S. who was supported to fight the invading Russians. He became the living example of all the wrongs done by America. America helped Laden directly or indirectly to procure arms and ammunition in lieu of drug money and to control large part of the World's drug trade. America has turned deaf ears when India time and again proved that Pakistan supplies the militants and terrorists in Afghanistan and India with arms, ammunition and moral support. When the U.S. was attacked it has again asked for help from Pakistan, which is the supporter of the Taliban and terrorists operating in India. Pakistan abetted Dawood Ibrahim a drug smuggler, Mafia don and the prime accused in the Bombay blasts, which killed hundreds in Bombay in 1993. It is really fascinating to see as how President Bush believes Pakistan President Pervez Musharraf who has gone on record and lied during the course of Agra Summit conference that Dawood Ibrahim was not in Pakistan whereas the facts say otherwise.

16

RAISING OF FUNDS

The collapse of the twin towers of the World Trade Center by the terrorists took many lives and ruined the families of the dead. In order to succor the families of the dead many prominent personalities and organizations came forward to raise funds. To raise funds of 50 millions dollars and distribute to the survivors and families of victims of Tuesday's terror attacks on New York city and Washington Mr. Michael Jackson, the pop singer known world-wide planned to record a new song titled "*what more can I give*". A two hours television extravaganza that brought together, some of the biggest names in entertainment raised $ 110 million for the victims of September 11 attacks attracting 59 million viewers on the 24th September. Former President, Bill Clinton and former Senator, Bob Dole contemplated to announce a drive to raise 100 million dollars to provide scholarships for children who lost their family members in the September 11 attacks.

Member of *Cirque Du Solell* performing at a benefit concert called, *Quebec/New Yorkers in Montreal* with over 100 artists including singer Celine Dion to help raise funds for the U.S. attack victims. Amidst 12,000 strong audience applauding at the Forum de Montreal Ice Hockey Stadium she belted out her single song *L' amour existe encore* (Love still exists).

To help raise money for victims, of the September 11 attacks on the World Trade Center fishermen from the Port town of Cordora

(U.S.) donated proceeds from two days worth of harvest to a fund raising campaign organized by the Anchorage fire fighters. The fish, totalling about 14.3 tones were sold on that day out of freezer vans parked at three-anchorage area grocery stores.

A line up that reads like a who's who of popular music over the past 30 years came together for a series of marathon concerts aimed at raising millions of dollars for the victims of September 11 attacks on the World Trade Center, the Pentagon and other places. Friends, rivals, golden oldies and teen bards shared the stage in New York City, on that day in a show of song and solidarity unseen since 1985. Dozens of stars from the movie, television and music industries took part in the emotional but subdued event providing entertainment and helping to answer telephones and to take pledges from viewers.

A large number of Indians go for work in the World Trade Center and it was feared that over 250 of them feared killed. Doctors of Indian origin in the U.S. were involved in treating victims of the terrorist attacks with more volunteering their services from the rest of the country.

Families of victims who died in the September 11 terrorist attacks were given the benefit of 5,00,000 dollars tax free from the federal government and 50,000 dollars of that upfront under interim regulations issued by the Special Master-Incharge of the funds.

17

AID TO PAKISTAN

A question arises why Pakistan supported the Taliban. Pakistan support for the Taliban official and unofficial stems from the fact that it had for the first time a pro-Pakistani Government in Afghanistan and the Pakistan has been supported by China, though Pakistan fear that of the Taliban's kind of Islam. However, the strategic factor that the need of Pakistan was for a reliable and dependent Government in Kabul with the terrorist factor linked indirectly.

After the declaration of war by President Bush, the Pakistan President Musharraf was literally caught between the devil of the Taliban and the deep sea of the U.S. Although Pakistan had always been the main prop of the Taliban, President Musharraf had to take the American side because otherwise America could devastate it militarily, politically and economically. He is cleverly diverting the subservient acts to the U.S. by saying that he was acting in the best interests of Pakistan and that his concerns for "freedom fighters" of Kashmir.

President Musharraf of Pakistan fearing that India wants to isolate them to move closer to the U.S. and get Pakistan declared as a terrorist State in their cause of Kashmir warned India to "lay off". He justified his action to support the U.S. stating that the planned actions were not directed against Islam or the people of Afghanistan but the Americans had three targets. Mr. Bin Laden (Al-Quaeda Movement), the Taliban and the International Terrorism.

India termed the remarks made by the President of Pakistan as unwarranted and emphatically stated that India do not have any animosity towards Islam and India has more Muslims than Pakistan. India's Ambassador to the U.S. further clarified that Islam is part of India's legacy and culture.

There were some apprehensions in India that Pakistan might have supported the U.S. on a condition that the U.S. should take an active role on Kashmir. A senior official of the National Security Council of the U.S. denied the above report and stated further that it has accepted "no condition and will not accept none from any country that wants to join in coalition against terrorism."

When terrorism turned New York into an inferno the political pandits in India thought that it was good for their own campaign against terrorism and bad for Pakistan. The eagerly anticipated great Indo-U.S. joint partnership against terrorism did not materialize as the Bush Administration turned to Pakistan which is placed better geographically to deal with the Taliban and Bin Laden.

The Pakistan establishment which feeds (and feeds off) the Jehad in Kashmir has now promptly junked its parents in Afghanistan soon after Mr. Bush declared war on terror. President Musharraf justified this being in the best interest of Pakistan. For him, as Jehad (in Kashmir) is vital and indispensable while the other of Laden and the Taliban is an embarrassment. In this context President Musharraf has already written off Laden because Pakistan comes first to him. In response of the support to the U.S. Pakistan expected a sizeable U.S. debt write off, the removal of sanctions, economic aid and some friendly noises over Kashmir. Political experts in the country suspect that the fundamental truth is that the Pakistan establishment is driven by a hatred of India, bitter moral outrage over Kashmir and the overwhelming desire not merely to avenge 1971 but to win at least one war against India. Islam comes next may be as a fuel for this fire of vengeance that emanates from the very heart of the military-bureaucratic establishment. They further suspect that Americans never build a coalition with predominantly Hindu India or an alliance of democracies when all their Islamic friends happens to be totalitarian States and monarchies. They further suggest that as the America and its allies sort out Laden we must just watch and see the development.

Pakistan attracted economic and military sanctions after a military coup in October, 1999 by President Musharraf who threw the democratically elected government of Nawaz Sharif. After September 11, the U.S. has moved a step closer to allow the American President to waive the sanctions for a second consecutive year, if he reaches the conclusion that such a step would help Pakistan's march towards democracy.

Haunted by the hard-liners at home and outside pressure from the U.S. to cooperate in launching an attack on Afghanistan, President Musharraf started playing Indian card by asking concession from the U.S. on Kashmir issue and insisted that India and Israel should be kept out of any military action against Pakistan. Pakistan which has been subjected to a range of economic sanctions since 1990 made the U.S. to lift them. The Taliban which was enjoying the support of Pakistan threatened to attack it as President Musharraf allowed the U.S. military forces to be stationed in Pakistan to raid against Bin Laden and his Taliban protectors.

Having sold the Taliban for fistful of dollars President Musharraf put a brave face swearing they will be short strapped and targeted. To the smiling, Pakistan who live recklessly and behaved arrogantly the waiver of sanctions by the U.S. means that the over-due foreign loans of thirty five billion dollars will be for all practical purpose would be written off with shipment of supplies resumed.

The U.S. approach to Pakistan for cooperation against Afghanistan based terrorists and the Pakistan response has complex implication for India. Mr. Musharraf despite opposition form extremist Islamic organizations with in his own country, has offered support to the U.S. has accepted the U.S. demand to allow Pakistan airspace and territory to be used for anti-terrorist operations. The only pre-condition stipulated was that operation launched form Pakistan territory should be multi-national force. He has agreed to close down the Afghanistan and Pakistan borders and stop essential supplies to the Taliban Government. He has already sent special diplomatic mission to Kandhar to ask the Taliban to extradite Bin Laden. He has demanded first that India and Israel should be kept out of the U.S. led anti-terrorist coalition. He also conveyed that the Jehad struggle in Jammu and Kashmir should be excluded from the Kashmir dispute. Apart from this he has demanded lifting of sanctions against Pakistan and asked for either writing off or delaying Pakistan's foreign debt repayments.

Driven by his need to cement ties with Pakistan in the hunt for Laden, President Bush has lifted whatever remained of the 1998 post-nuclear-test economic sanctions on both India and Pakistan. Reacting to the above development Finance Minister Yashwant Sinha said that "except for certain defence supplies sanctions have no meaning. I do not think this as a development of earth-shaking importance". The Indian officials, however, added that "we are not bothered whether the sanctions are lifted or not though Pakistan would benefit enormously as it is in tight spot".

The U.S. Government in order to please Pakistan signed an agreement rescheduling $ 379 million Government to Government debt owed by Islamabad to Washington. Reacting sharply to Western media reports that the U.S. decision to lift sanctions against India was a reward the External Affairs ministry made it clear that India has been engaged in a war against terrorism for well over a decade now and 53,000 families of innocents were the sufferers of this terrorism in the country. The Ministry has further clarified that a largest democracy, needs no rewards for the stand it takes on issues of principle. Some political observers in India cautioned that the U.S. is some what like the village money lender who gives much needed loan and trap the poor nations and trap them in their iron vice of interest repayment leading to penury. In 1974 Bangladesh which had been receiving food aid from the U.S. under PL 480 to face the famine insisted by the U.S. to restrict its exports of jute to Cuba. Bangladesh eventually had to fall in line and became an instrument of settling the U.S. political scores with Cuba.

Pakistan was tracing for a possible biological attack by Mr.

Laden's network and the Taliban after American defence officials warned Islamabad of such a danger. Pakistan authorities also sought one million dollar assistance from the U.S. to upgrade its medical and laboratory facilities as they have got the required expertise in preparing the vaccine for biological agents and if funds were provided it could be made available in days.

In a major diplomatic initiative Chinese President Jiang Zemin has announced an aid of 1.21 million dollars for Pakistan and fully backed President Musharraf's efforts to combat terrorism.

London based *Jane's Intelligence Review* has said Pakistan ISI remains the key to providing accurate information to the U.S led alliance in its war against Bin Laden and his Taliban hosts as it controls the army of "Islam" comprising Laden's Al-Qaeda and Kashmir militants. It is well known that Jaish and Taliban share the umbilical cord with the Jamait-e-Ulma-i-Islam in Pakistan and thus Jaish represents the sentiments of anger witnessed on the streets of Pakistan against Musharaff's alliance with Washington.

After the World Trade Center and the Pentagon tragedies and in the hope of getting military and intelligence cooperation in Afghanistan the US has lionized Musharaff showering with a corncupia of economic aid-no strings attached-that has included 600 million dollars in immediate cash infusions, 2.1 billion dollars in projected grants and credits, 1.5 million dollars in international monetary fund credits which was blocked by the U.S. earlier and a rescheduling of 12.2 billion dollars in Pakistan's debt to a US led consortium of aid donors (including 3.75 billion dollars owned directly to the U.S.)

There is an old adage saying that folly of one man will be fortune of another. Overzealous with their bigotry-act Laden and Omar lost control of Afghanistan. Seizing the opportunity President Musharaff with his diplomatic skill garnered millions of dollars aid to Pakistan from the U.S.A. and others.

18

AFGHANISTAN – THE TALIBAN

Afghanistan is geographically surrounded by Iran, Turkmenistan, Uzbekistan, Tajikistan, China and Pakistan. In the earlier years it became an invasion route for Alexander, Chengiz Khan, Tairmur Lung, the Turks, the Lodhis and Babur. Three fourths of Afghanistan has been hit by drought for two years now and only 12 percent land is arable. There is little food to eat without any substantial aid. Though they lack food they are the world's largest growers of poppy with an annual production of about 1,670 metric tonnes.

Afghanistan was ruled by Pastun ruler, Ahmed Shah Durrani from 1747 to 1773 and anarchy persisted from 1826-1933. In 1973 there was a military coup led by Prime Minister Mohammad Daoud who dethroned King Zahir and Afghanistan became a republic. In 1979, the Russians with a view to subjugate Afghanistan and rule through their puppet regime entered Afghanistan with a hundred thousands troops along with the modern weapons. The Afghans waged a continuous war against Russians for almost a decade. The U.S. supported when they were fighting against Russia and supplied stringers and launchers to contain the communism. After five years President Daoud was killed and Babrak Kamal became the new leader with the help of USSR and he ruled the country for the next nine years. Mohammad Nejbullah became the President of Afghanistan in 1987. He ruled the country for about four years and when the Soviet troops withdrew from Afghanistan he was ousted in 1992. In his place Burhanuddin Rabbani was elected for a two year term. Then in 1996 the Taliban seized Kabul and hanged Najibullah. The family of Afghan President Najibullah, who was propped by Russia and was executed by the Talibans were living in Delhi behind high walls of a house and they were pinning hopes on the U.S. to restore some semblance of order in the country.

Since 1996 the Afghans are living under the oppressive rule of the Taliban that imposed strict religious codes and made them to live in isolation with starvation and exhaustion always staring at them. Afghanistan is a very backward country with a population of 25 million people with 64 percent illiterates. Seventy percent of the people are under-nourished and at an average, men do not live beyond 40 years and women 44. One fourth of children die before reaching the age of five and only 12 percent has access to safe drinking water.

A few years ago the United Nations estimated that there are 500,000 disabled orphans, millions of widows of the approximately two million men killed during the war with the Soviets. The Taliban and Bin Laden are not Afghans. They are not even the Government of Afghanistan. The Taliban are a cult of ignorant psychotics who captured Afghanistan in 1996 and have been holding the country in bondage ever since.

In November 1994 General Naseerullah Babar, Pakistan's then interior Minister sought to seize control of Pakistan's Afghan policy from ISI. In this search, he was aided by Maulana Fazl-Ur-Rehman of the Jamaat-E-Uleema-E-Islami who was a coalition partner of Benazir Bhutto. Fazl-Ur-Rehman sourced Mullah Omar from one of his 20,000 Madrasas and convinced General Babar that Omar would be the most plaint proxy and all the revenues from drug traffiking would flow in the direction of the PPP as opposed to the ISI. Adequately armed, on October 12, 1994 a small force of a few hundred Taliban (students) from Pakistan Madrassas took control of the town of Spin Boldak from Hekmatyar's men. In such a way the Taliban was born and undoubtedly it was a creation of Pakistan. Further, it was commander Masood who was impressed by Bin Laden's capabilities in the war against Soviets in 1980 persuaded Prince Turki Bin Faisal, head of the Istakhbarat to convince Bin Laden to relocate himself in Afghanistan. Thereafter Bin Laden and Mullah Omar came together to such an extent that they developed personal relationship through ties of marriage. Mullah Omar is merely a figure head and Bin Laden took over the executive responsibilities of the Taliban by the time the U.S. declared war on terror.

Afghanistan was known world-wide as a major supplier of drugs and in the wake of reports that the Taliban was short strapped for funds with war looming large, it was looking to flush the drug-market with its goods to raise money for its operations. Senior Police officials of Gujarat say that brown sugar, charas, heroin were among the narcotic items that land in the State enroute other nations from countries like Afghanistan a major supplier and producer of contraband. Many facts about the mafia must be read together to get a perspective on the situation as it applies to terrorism. First the drug mafia girdles the globe from South America to South-East Asia. Second, Afghanistan is the world's biggest production center for drugs after South America. Third, drug trafficking was an established means to fund raising for political militants.

Laden may be too orthodox a Muslim to approve the drugs. But the business needs it as much as the drug lords need him. Pakistan has disowned its own child the Taliban at an hour of crisis of retaliation by the U.S. and the U.K. President Musharaff not only turned his back on the Taliban but without any reservations denounced them as harbourers of terrorists and claims all this was necessary to protect the Kashmir cause. The betrayal by Pakistan and revenge is going to be a bigger issue for the Taliban.

Because of terror attacks in the World Trade Center, Pentagon and other areas, the U.S. wanted Bin Landen dead or alive. In retalisation, the U.S. backed by several other countries declared war and bombed incessantly many areas of Afghanistan to flush out Bin Laden and Omar. Fearing the U.S. strikes tens of thousands of Afghans moved out of Afghanistan in search assistance and safety as refugees. After twenty years of brutal fighting and three years of severe drought the fate of thousands of Afghanistan women has become very miserable since the Taliban captured Kabul on 27th September 1996. The Taliban regime has imposed a string of social and economic, cultural and economic restrictions on the women, as they are forbidden to work outside their home, must wear *Burqa* when going out. Girls are banned from attending schools and universities. According to Nancy Dupree, an Afghan scholar all these restrictions imposed by the Taliban regime are alien to the true spirit of Islam. According to the above scholar, Islam emphasizes equality, justice and education for both men and women. When the Taliban took over the reigns of Afghanistan twenty five percent of Government employees were women. Tens of thousands of widows and disabled men became heads of families and were shouldering the responsibility by employing themselves in different organizations. They were forced by the Talibans to surrender their jobs even if they were the sole earning members of their families.

It is interesting to note, Aisha the beloved wife of the Prophet never wore a veil and covered her face. The Prophet severely admonished when some families grumbled over the issue. As a matter of fact, Aisha led an army after the death of the Prophet and fought fiercely against the forces of Ali. The attitude of the Taliban regime in treating all their women as.domestic servants would have been abhorred by the Prophet. Proscribing the Muslims women or any other women in the civilized world exposing their curved limbs is tolerable but compelling them to wear *Burqa* while going in the streets is distasteful.

Afghanistan has always been overwhelmingly Muslim but until the upheaval of the early 1990's when ethnic militia fought bloody street battles in Kabul, Sikhs, Hindus and Jews played a large role in the economy. Many left to escape the fighting. But for those who stayed on the hardline Islamic fundamentalism that the Taliban introduced when they swept into Kabul in 1996, they were forced to worship behind closed doors. The Taliban ordered the Sikhs and Hindus to wear yellow patches on their clothes to mark themselves as non-Muslims. As they could not freely practice their religion and the women had to stay indoors all the time their pinning hopes to for formation of a broad-based Afghanistan government where minorities are well protected has vanished.

After the defeat and departure of the Soviets from Afghanistan, Pakistan took the opportunities to put to use the surplus arms left by America as an arsenal for the Taliban and Kashmiri militants and launched the Taliban to come to power in Afghanistan.

Prominent Baluch and Sindh leaders have flayed the successive governments in Pakistan for toeing the ISI policy of supporting fundamentalist forces in Afghanistan that made the war-ravaged country the epicentre of terrorism in the world. They said that the military regime of Pakistan thrived on policies of religious nationalism and urged the U.S. the military regime to restore democracy in Pakistan.

19

ATTACK ON INDIAN PARLIAMENT

The fear of war was felt in India when Shri Atal Behari Vajpayee did some plain speaking while addressing a series of public meetings after the attacks warned the country to prepare for harsh economic measures and called off his visit to New York to attend the U.N General Assembly session. He said that a crisis was looming large over the world's horizon and there can be a war anywhere and in any form. Sensing the danger of terror attack the Indian Government has also set up country's first ever Integrated Defence Staff.

With the anti-Taliban Northern Alliance offering cooperation to the U.S., India has got a shot in the arm in its diplomatic initiatives against Pakistan. The over-throw of the Taliban regime in Afghanistan will serve as a big boost to its crusade against terrorism in Kashmir. Anti-Taliban regime will not be under the control of Pakistan. Senior military officials say that the problem which has been faced with for so many years was now being recognized throughout the world following the September 11 terrorist attacks in New York and Washington.

The U.S. has assured New-Delhi after a fortnight of terrorist attacks and during the visit of National Security Advisor Mr. Brajesh Mishra that its global drive to combat the menace also covered

Jammu and Kashmir and would not rest till it goes after every terrorist group and the countries harboring them. They also made it clear that there would be no change in the Indo-U.S. relationship in the wake of the U.S. seeking Pakistan's support for military operations against Laden and his network in Afghanistan.

The fundamentalist terrorism in Pakistan and Afghanistan has been menacing not only India but Central Asian Republics like Tejikistan and Uzbekistan threatening their very secular fabric. It is also Russia's enemy. What the U.S.A has now experienced has been experienced by India in Bombay (1993) and countless times in Delhi and Kashmir. Nearly 50,000 civilians have perished in Kashmir. Lakhs of people not all Hindus have left Kashmir for fear of their lives and woman cannot live there in freedom. The difference today is that America tasted it first hand and can relate to India's experience as never before.

Gujarat is a major transit point for shipment of drugs to the West, South Asia and the South East Asia. The Security agencies in India were, therefore put on high alert in Gujarat to check landing of any contraband.

The Government of India, a week later of terrorist attacks banned the radical Islamic outfit Students Islamic Movement of India (SIMI) for alleged anti-National activities and launched a major crack down in ten States arresting over a hundred of its activists. The two year ban was notified by the Home Ministry under the unlawful activities (prevention) Act 1967 after Uttar Pradesh, Maharashtra and Madhya Pradesh have proposed for banning in the wake of involvement of SIMI activities in communal violence in Kanpur, Pune and some other States.

The Prime Minister of India assured all the major political parties of the country that India has not given any assurance to the U.S. directly or indirectly of making available its air bases in any action against Afghanistan and made it clear that it was not dependent on anyone in its fight against terrorism. While America and its allied forces were preparing to attack Laden and his followers in Afghanistan, the militants with a suicide bomber on 1st October rammed a Tata Sumo packed with explosives right into the main gate of the heavily fortified Assembly building of Jammu and Kashmir killing 38 people. The Jaish-e-Mohammad, the group floated by Pakistan based Moulana Masood Azhar said it was behind the attack and even identified the bomber as Wajahat Hussain of Pakistan's North-West Frontier province.

Chief Minister Farooq Abdullah with tears rolling down his cheeks urged the Prime Minister on 3rd October to ensure that the militant training camps in Pakistan Occupied Kashmir are smashed, so that the misery of the people comes to an end. He said, "this war is 12 years old and the Kashmiris are very unfortunate to have been caught in the fire of two countries. One is targeting us and the other is not defending against the aggression unleased by the former".

Contrary to conventional wisdom, Jaish-e-Mohammad's suicide attack on the Jammu and Kashmir Assembly in which thirty-eight innocent people were killed was much a warning to Islamabad for its role in the current International Compaign against, the Taliban as it was a message to New Delhi.

The Jaish-e-Mohammad which first claimed responsibility and then, apparently under pressure from Pakistan issued a denial after a full day later. Mr.Abudllah said that India was not against Pakistan, but it was Pakistan, the ISI and the Hurriyat who were whipping up passions against Hindus and India. Soon after the attack on the Assembly building of Jammu and Kashmir, India has told the U.S that its patience is wearing thin with Pakistan's support to terrorism in Kashmir and virtually served notice that it will be compelled to take its own steps to combat the menace.

The strong Indian message conveyed in an unprecedented letter from the Prime Minister Vajpayee to the U.S. President Bush brought personally to a meeting of External Affairs Minister Jaswant Singh had at the White House with National Security Adviser Condoleeze Rice, where President Bush stayed for 40 minutes during which the two sides went over the situation arising from September

11 attacks especially in the light of the latest outrage in Kashmir. Emerging from the White House Mr. Singh told reporters that the President "was kind enough to share his thought and there was agreement that the fight against terrorism cannot be unidimensional or unidirectional".

The British Prime Minister Tony Blair after meeting the Pakistan President Musharraf in Pakistan after terrorist attack met the Prime Minister of India at the end of first week of October at New Delhi and made it clear that Pakistan and Afghanistan are both epicenters of terrorism and the menace has become global one and its solution too must be global and should not be dealt in isolation. However, Prime Minister Vajpayee praised Mr. Blair's active role in building and strengthening the global coalition against terrorism and his warning against equating terrorism with Islam.

Here in India, between 50,000 to 70,000 civilians had died due to terrorism in the name of religious faiths and 300,000 Hindus had been terrorized to flee from their homes in Kashmir valley. The terrorists in India and America or elsewhere don't live in their homes or sleep on the streets and move arms and RDX. They are harboured, hosted and entertained by the people who incite and sympathize them in the name of religion and ideology. The Taliban and Pakistan were the best examples where Bin Laden, Dawood Ibrahim respectively were living luxuriously running their nefarsious activities.

Despite all-round condemnation of terrorist attacks in Jammu and Kashmir, Pakistan termed what was happening there as "Freedom Struggle" more so after President Musharraf condemned the 1st October blast at Jammu and Kashmir Assembly in Srinagar. Americans have rightly perceived that September 11 attack was on their way of life and value system and not just destruction of massive structure of the World Trade Center. In the same way India should pursue the Kashmir issue not as a fight for a piece of land but for the unity and preservation of very concept of India. There is no doubt that Kashmir is always a part of cultural, emotional and civilizational unity of India, apart from the fact that Instrument of Accession was signed by their ruler of the State under the Indian Independence Act 1947, which also created Pakistan.

As a matter of fact the history of democracy in India tolerating even anti-national viewpoints of Hurriyat leaders, inciting the Muslims to support Bin Laden by no less then a person like the Shahi Imam of Jama Masjid, is as good as any in the world. In contrast the U.S. which claims to be the champion of democracy when felt harming them has got five of its main T.V channels to stop broadcasting speech unedited because it was nothing but propaganda.

In so far as the battle in Kashmir is concerned strongly it is between Pakistan belief that religion is the basis of State-hood and what India and the undivided State of Jammu and Kashmir opted for in 1947 a multi cultural, multi faith society. If India concedes the persistence demand of separation just because majority of the population in the valley are Muslims it would not only a suicidal decision inviting trouble for the 150 millions of Muslims spread over in all parts of the country but would be the beginning of the end of India as an entity.

After September 11 terrorist attacks on the U.S. it became necessary for the Union Cabinet of India to approve the promulgation of an ordinance to combat terrorism in place of scrapped TADA making non-disclosure of information relating to a terrorist act as an offence etc. To divert the attention of the World, Pakistan based militant outfit Lash-Kare-Toiba has threatened to launch suicide attacks against India. In the first one year they carried out nearly fifty suicide attacks. In order to flush out Laden and to avenge the terrorist attacks on the World Trade Center, the Pentagon and other places President Bush has given massive military and economic aid to Pakistan. Well aware of the hypocrisy of Pakistan, Democratic Congresswoman Nita Lowery warned the Bush Government that Pakistan might use military components against India. An utterly dirty sight for India as anything that is benefit to Pakistan is loss to India.

The simple fact is that Pakistan had invaded Kashmir and the Indian Army had gone to Kashmir but not to invade Kashmir. They were sent on the express invitation of the Maharaja and Sheik Abdullah. Kashmir is a Hindu State with the majority of its people being Muslims. After the attack on Jammu and Kashmir Assembly in Srinagar, President Musharaf was compelled to call it as terrorism and condemn the act. The U.S which is waging war against terrorism understood to have asked Islamabad to hand over to India, Dawood Ibrahim, Tiger Memon and other accused in the Bombay blast case who have taken shelter in Pakistan.

While the attention of the whole world was concentrated on the developments of war in Afghanistan five terrorists carrying deadly explosives and weapons in a camera bag drove in a stolen white Ambassador car with the Home Ministry car label and flashing a red beacon stormed the Parliament House of India on the forenoon of 13th December. On this fateful day both Houses adjourned at 11.05 a.m. and around two hundred Members of Parliament started to leave Parliament House. The terrorists who hoodwinked the security guards by driving into Parliament in a white Ambassador with red beacon flashing and siren wailing entered into Parliament House at 11-40 a.m. and started firing indiscriminately at Gate No.2 and few minutes later at Gate Nos 12 and 8. The then Vice-President, Krishna Kant had providential escape as his departure for home was delayed by few minutes. The drama lasted for fifty minutes leading to fourteen causalities - nine security personnel and five terrorists (including a suicide bomber "fidayee" of terrorist group who blowed himself up).

Fortunately Shri Atal Behari Vajpayee, the Prime Minister of India, Shri L.K.Advani, Home Minister and Mrs.Sonia Gandhi, Opposition Leader were not present in the House at the time of the incident. Unable to bear the menace of terrorism in India, the Prime Minister declared war against terrorism on the 13th December terming terrorism has entered the last phase and should be fought in a decisive manner. The Prime Minister addressing a meeting of Confederation of Indian Industries in Kolkata termed the attack on

Parliament as an attempt to wipe out the political leadership and bring turmoil in the country. He said that the terrorist acts on Indian soil have transgressed the limits of patience of the Indian people and assured the nation that such attacks will be repulsed.

The Delhi Police after thorough investigation confirmed that the five militants killed while trying to storm the Parliament House were all Pakistanis and active J-e-m members. They were Mohammad, the group leader, Hamza Haider alias Tufial, Rana and Raja. The arrest of Delhi University lecturer Syed Abdul Rahman Geelani and his subsequent interrogation revealed that he along with Mohd. Afzal and Shaukat Hussain Guru, both residents of Sopore in Baremullah district of Jammu and Kashmir had been in constant touch with the five militants of Jaish-e-Mohammad and planned to storm the Parliament House on 13th September with the active support of Laskar-e-Toiba and at the instigation of Pakistan ISI.

A year after the terrorist attack on Parliament the Delhi Court on 16th December, 2002 convicted Mohd.Afzal Shaukat, Hussain Guru and SAR Geelani under prevention of Terrorism Act (POTA) who found to be guilty of criminal conspiracy, "with the intention to kill the Prime Minister, Home Minister and to make hostage all the Members of Parliament in Parliament. Describing the attack on Indian Parliament as a"rarest of rare case" the special court imposed the death sentence to the above three accused on 18th December, 2002 under POTA as well as under section 302 of the IPC for the murder of nine security personnel. While pronouncing the Judge stated that they were"inspired by Bin Laden and Masood Azhar. It is anybody's guess as, how the higher courts would decide their fate when they go for appeal.

Five days after the attack on Parliament the Cabinet Committee on Security was weighing options to strike at terrorist camps in Pakistan Occupied Kashmir. However, Indian and Pakistani troops continued to exchange fire at several points along the international border. When the matter has come up for discussion, the opposition parties pledged full support and the Government got the carte blanche it sought from Parliament to go on the offensive against Pakistan. Surprisingly the sleuths were convinced that the militants had contacts in Dubai, Pakistan and Germany.

Accusing Pakistan of not taking any action against the terrorist groups behind the December 13 attack, India announced immediate recall of their High Commissioner and the termination of the Samjhauta express and the two year old Lahore bus with effect from 1st January of 2002. These steps not only deepened the chill in bilateral relations, they also put pressure on the Washington-Islamabad coalition in their compaign in Afghanistan.

India has also notched a major diplomatic victory with the President Bush announcing his decision to cut financing for Laskhar-e-Toiba calling it a "Satateless sponsor of terrorism. President Bush while condemning the attack on Parliament blamed the L-e-T saying it "was only the most recent attack on the institution of Indian democracy". The day the U.S. clamped down on the L-e-T, the militants killed three Sikh girls in Poshkora village in Srinagar. President Bush also banned the Ummah Taneer-e-Nau. The UTN has been founded in the year 2001, by Basheeruddin Mehmood former Director for nuclear power at the Pakistan Atomic Energy Commission.

While the matter stood thus, Indian and Pakistani troops traded fire at various border outposts in Jammu, Kathua districts, Saichan and Kargil sectors and the Prime Minister of India asserted that India is well-versed in the art of war. In a desperate attempt with no other alternative the militants killed six innocent women in Anantnag of Jammu and Kashmir. As a retaliatory measure, the Indian troops destroyed twentyone Pakistani bunkers, two ammunition dumps and about 25 Pakistani troops were severely injured.

New Delhi achieved a major diplomatic break through when the Pakistan Government freezed the assets of the militant Islamic outfit, Lashkar-e-Toiba as a follow-up move to a similar action by the U.S. In a major break through self styled deputy chief of Pakistan based L-e-T outfit Saifullah Askari alias Owais along with the close aide Mirza alias Abu Ali were killed by Special Operation Groups of Jammu and Kashmir police in Baramulla District. On the 24th of December, twenty-two Pakistani soldiers were killed and atleast twenty-five bunkers destroyed in retaliatory fire by Indian troops in the Karmara and Keri areas across the LOC in Poonch District of Jammu and Kashmir.

A staff member of the High Commission of Pakistan, was caught red-handed while collecting sensitive documents from a Parliament Official of India. He was asked to leave India within seven days. Pakistan has also redeployed nuclear capable medium range ballistic missile batteries on the 22nd December and moved its troops and Air Force closer to the Sindh Rajasthan and Punjab borders. On the fourth consecutive day of exchange of fire between India and Pakistan forces, the Defence sources said thirteen Pakistani soldiers were killed and eighteen of their bunkers destroyed by the Indain troops along the LOC in the Jammu-Poonch sector.

The Northern Alliance troopers sifting through piles of papers found in the Rishkor rubble South of Kabul said that there was enough evidence to suggest that many Pakistanis and Arabs were trained there for missions in Kashmir. The same sources said that beneath the rubble there was probably more secrets still awaiting to be disclosed.

Turning more heat on Pakistan, the U.S. on the 26th December branded Pakistani-based L-e-T and J-e-M as terrorist outfits for their involvement in the attacks on Indian Parliament and Jammu and Kashmir State Assembly and wished to work with India and Pakistan to "shut" them down.

The Govt. of India stepped up its offensive against Pakistan on 27th December with a set of tough diplomatic measures sending a strong signal of its dissatisfaction with the steps taken by Islamabad so far against L-e-T and J-e-M. The strength of the High Commission in New Delhi and Islamabad has been slashed reducing the number of personnel from the agreed limit of 110 to 55. Those who remained were not allowed to move out of the municipal limits of Delhi. In addition, India has banned all over flights by Pakistani aircraft, including commercial flights of the Pakistan International Airlines. Pakistan also responded against India with tit-for-tat sanctions and reduced to have India's diplomatic staff in Islamabad and banned Indian overflights. Amid growing Indo-Pak tensions the U.S. President, Bush and the French President Jacques Chirac spoke to Prime Minister Vajpayee on 29th December 2001 and discussed the latest situation in the wake of mutual sanctions slapped by New Delhi and Islamabad.

India's war against terrorism has been code named as "Operation Sangram" to be conducted jointly by the three services. Troops and material mobilisation was complete by the end of December 2001. The Air force expected to play a greater role in its joint operations. The Govt.'s diplomatic offensive against Pakistan was endorsed by the Opposition leaders at an all party meeting convened by the Prime Minister on the 30th December. And in a move that underlines how political differences have been sunk on the issue of National Security, all party delegations visited important World capitals to compaign against Pakistan sponsored terrorism.

The Home Minister L.K.Advani said that "the war is on, if not declared but definitely covert". The day before he left for the SAARC Summit, Prime Minister rejected the demand of Pakistan for more evidence against the terrorists involved in the attack on Parliament as meaningless exercise. "The five bodies in the Parliament complex and the papers recovered from them have established that they were Pakistan Nationals."

On the eve of the SARRC Summit the Indo-Pak chill deepened with a fresh round in the war of words. The External Affairs Minister of India slammed Pakistan for making "lame excuses and taking no action against terrorists wanted by India over a decade. In a toughening of stand the Minister also ripped apart Pakistan Officials statement as reported in *the New York Times* on 2-1-02 that it would only provide "moral and diplomatic support" to groups based in Jammu and Kashmir. "How can moral support be provided to immoral activity like terrorism" he said.

In a special gesture, Pakistan President Musharaf walked upto Prime Minister Vajpayee on the 5th of January 2002 during the course of the SAARC summit and offered his "hand of sincere friendship" and shook hands with him. Shri.Vajpayee appeared to be momentarily surprised as President Musharaf walked across the elevated dais at the inaugural ceremony towards the Indian leader who then responded with a suppressed smile, got up and shook hands to the applause of the SAARC leaders and rest of the gathering. This was the first encounter between the two leaders after the dead locked Agra summit.

For the first time drawing no distinction between terrorism and freedom struggle, Pakistan President Musharaff said on 12th January,2002 that terrorism has no place in the Kashmir cause. And as a part of package of social and religious reforms unprecedented in Pakistan's history, he banned L-e-T and J-e-M declaring a virtual Jehad against the "Jehadis".

The highlights of Pakistan President Musharaff address to his nation on the 12th Jan. 2002 were

1) Banned L-e-T and J-e-M.
2) Ruled out handing over of Pakistanis wanted by India.
3) Wished to take appropriate action against non-Pakistani's wanted by India.
4) Warned India against crossing of the borders.
5) Offered fresh dialogue with the Prime Minister of India on Kashmir.
6) Not to allow its territory for terrorist activities.
7) Banned extremist groups Sipah-e-Sahaba, Tehrik-e-Jafria, Tehrik-e-Naifaz-e-Shariat.
8) All Madrasas to be registered by March end 2002.
9) Any group found involved in December 13 attack on the Indian Parliament and 1st October attack on the Jammu & Kashmir Assembly to be dealt suitably.

On 13th January, India indicated its willingness to give Pakistan

President Musharaff a chance with a cautious positive response to his bold commitment on the terrorism issue. The Govt. of India was willing to give more time to Pakistan to fulfil its promises on ending cross-border terrorism.

Political Pandits in India, however, had misgivings of President Musharaff's speech. They questioned, can India afford to trust Gen.Musharaff whose fear of the U.S. shall override his hatred for India. The history of past three years offered little comfort.

The then Pakistan Prime Minister Nawaz Sharif went out of his way to pick General Musharaff as the Chief of Pakistan army. His reward was a coup followed by exile. Not long back Gen. Musharaff appeared on the BBC lauding the Taliban, an organization which the Pakistan Army had solicitously nursed. It took just 24 hours for the General to stab his child in the back. If that was how this man treated his friends, should India hope for any better treatment. Further when, Pakistan said that there were no longer any Indian criminals in their country wanted by India, it appeared to be literally correct as the Dawood Ibrahims and the Tiger Memon were told to move out of Pakistan a day before the General's speech.

A day after top American officials arrived in Delhi to work out ways to fight terrorism with their counterparts and hours before the FBI Chief began his official engagements in New-Delhi, the American Center in Kolkota's Chowringee area was sprayed by as many as fifty-four bullets on the early morning of 22nd January 2002 killing four policemen. Four gunmen on two motorcycles fired AK-47 and injured fourteen people including twelve policemen infront of the high walled building that houses the U.S. consulate's public affair section and the Library. After spraying the bullets the gunmen fled. The U.S. center attackers at Kolkota, Mohammad Idris alias Wajid alias Zahid, a resident of Sakin Khannewal in Pakistan and Mohd. Salim, a resident of Punjab were killed in a police encounter in Hazaribagh in Jharkhand on 28th January. Both of them confessed the crime to the police before they breathed last.

Aftab Ansari alias Farhan Malik who was caught in Dubai and transported to New-Delhi had admitted on 10th February 2002 to having carried out the American Center attack at Kolkata in order to revenge the killing of Arif Raza Khan in a police encounter. He had further admitted to the kidnapping of Khadim's Partha Roy Burman, the coal merchant, Anand Agarwal in Benaras and Niranjan Shah in Mumbai. Farhan Malik and his accomplice were taken to Gujarat for the investigation.

After about 27 months of attack on Indian Parliament, Javed Ashraf Qazi who was the ISI Chief from 1993-1995 during Benazir Bhutto's second Government made a very significant statement in the Pakistan Parliament on 5th March, 2004 admitting that Jaish-e-Mohammed was behind the Parliament attack of December, 13, 2001, as well as the death of "Thousands of Kashmiris"

"We must not be afraid of admitting that Jaish was involved in the death of thousands of innocent Kashmiris bombing the Indian Parliament, Daniel Pearl's murder and attempts on President Musharraf.

20

BIOLOGICAL AND CHEMICAL WEAPONS

A British Foreign Office Minister said that the Al-Qaeda network has been trying to get hold of biological and chemical weapons for the last ten years. This warning came after a tabloid newspaper editor in Florida was killed with strain of anthrax.

The fear of anthrax appeared in the U.S. and in populations around the world. The U.S. defence officials believed, that Laden's Al-Qaeda terrorist network in Afghanistan had developed chemical and biological weapons. The chemical weapons the Al-Qaeda is believed to possess include simple poison weapons such as chlorine and phosgene. As far as, biological weapons, the Al-Qaeda network might have developed some type of deadly toxin weapons including Anthrax.

America which is in the grip of biological warfare feared that it could kill more people than the terrorists with hijacked planes on Sept.11. There was one death in Florida. The FBI feared that thirtyfive male students who sought job placement assistance from Denver Truck School might be used in future either with traditional explosive or with hazardous or chemical cargo.

A seventh-month-old became the victim of anthrax. In Florida a second employee of "Sun" tabloid in Boca Raton tested positive of anthrax. The United States, France and Canada were reeling under the fear of anthrax. One of the reasons why the Americans were so terror striken by the spate of anthrax-laden letters and few deaths was the lack of fool-proof vaccine, against the disease. Though there is a vaccine, it is now available only to the U.S. defence personnel. But now researchers from the Ohio State University Columbus, U.S.A., have reported that a new DNA based vaccine developed by their team could be effective against human anthrax. Twentynine people were exposed to anthrax from a letter containing white powder that was addressed to the U.S. Senator, Tom Daschle. To ward off the evil, the U.S. Government offered one million dollars reward for information leading to the arrest and conviction of those responsible for mailing anthrax.

To avoid any danger of exposing to anthrax, China has banned all mail packages containing white powder from entering or exiting the country in response to the on going anthrax scare. With fortyfive cases of anthrax infection and exposure emerging in the U.S. after weeks of Sept.11 attacks investigators were searching frantically to the source.

While the U.S. forces launched a three pronged attack on the key city of Mazar-e-Sharif, reports have reached Washington that two postal workers have died of inhalation of anthrax, two more hospitalized and nine others were monitored with suspicious symptoms. Anthrax culture has been found at the remote military facility where all mail for the White House was screened. Anthrax has claimed a fourth victim in the U.S. and spores were detected at a post office in Kanas city of Missouri that handled mail from the U.S. capital of Washington. Anthrax spores were found in another U.S. government building as post offices in California were being tested for the disease.

The Pentagon post office serves thousands of civilian and military workers at the sprawling headquarters of the U.S. military across the Potomao River from Washington in Arlington, Virginia. Surprisingly anthrax was found in the above post office. In order to save themselves from the biological warfare most of the Americans are taking steps to protect from anthrax.

21

DECLARATION OF WAR

The war has begun on the 7th of October,2001. The U.S. and U.K. launched a series of attacks on three major cities of Afghanistan and the missisles destroyed Kandhar Airport, the training bases of the Taliban and the house of Mullah Omar. The heart of Afghanistan was pounded by 15 bombers, 25 strike aircraft and 50 cruise missiles.

Seizing the opportunity of the U.S. and U.K. bombings, the Northern Alliance forces unleashed an onslaught on the 9th October to capture the capital of Afghanistan. Russia which promised to fight terrorism began to deliver weapons to the Northern Alliance.

Justifying its action of bombing to the U.N., the U.S. led forces hit the Afghan city of Kandahar on the 9th October though the Taliban claimed that private houses were hit near Kabul Airport and women and children were killed. Fear gripped in thousands of Kabul residents and afraid of more U.S. attacks, they left the Afghan capital.

In response to the U.S. President Bush request the Canadian Prime Minister agreed to send more than 2000 Canadian military personnel to fight in Afghanistan. Chinese President Jiang Zemin expressing his support to the U.S. led fight against terrorism cautioned against the civilian targets.

On the third day of the attack, the U.S. fighter jets rained bombs on Kabul, Kandahar and Herat. Though they attacked Mullah Omar house, he was safe. The American planes heavily bombed the Mewand area expecting that Laden might be hiding there. The missiles have also killed four U.N. workers. While the Northern Alliance troops captured strategically Panjikarla in the Samangan Province, President Musharaf pleaded for the inclusion of the Talibans in a broad based future Government in Kabul for fear of guerilla war by the militia, if they are excluded.

The Taliban troops have also traded gunfire with Pakistan guards at Northern West Frontier Province and again withdrew to their own territory. China and Russia have expressed support for the formation of a broad based coalition government in place of the Taliban regime.

As the U.S. warplanes launched daynight attacks on the fourth successive day targeting Kandahar and Kabul, the Al-Qaeda network of Laden warned that the U.S. would face further attacks by hijacked planes and urged all Muslims in "Jehad" against America.

The U.S. jets launched heavy fresh attack on 12th October, causing earth shaking detonators in Kabul area shutting of electricity in the capital. In Kandahar the Qishla Jadeed military was attacked. Accidentally a U.S. jet missed the target and hit a civilian area in Kabul. The Northern Alliance which was fighting alongwith the U.S. led forces claimed victories of three villages within twenty kilometers of Aibak the capital of Samangan.

Inspite of loosing his two sons, several of his relatives wounded and huge plumes of smoke was engulfing Kabul and a part of Kandahar in the U.S. attacks Omar issued a scathing statement denouncing the American attacks and again emphasized that there was no move to "hand over anyone".

While the U.S. and U.K. forces were striking the strategic places of Afghanistan, President Bush gave second chance on 11th October, to hand over Laden which was laughed away and rejected by the Taliban leaders.

It appeared that on the very first night of the U.S. attacks in

Afghanistan, the American forces had Omar in their gun sights and failed to kill him as the rules of engagement was in effect on Sunday night and the CIA could not order such a strike. It has instead decided to target a few cars in front of the building to frighten Omar out of his premises. Moments after he left, the building was attacked and destroyed by the U.S. F-18 jets.

In the first week of the war the U.S. led forces hit Kabul Airport, air defence sites, radio transmission tower, the areas used for training and housing the Taliban troops, Kandahar airfield its air defence sites the Taliban Garrisons, compound of Omar, several terrorist camp in North of Kandahar, Mazar-E-Sharif air field, its Surface to Air missile site, two defence sites in and around northern city and as well as a concentration of the Taliban forces near the border with Uzbekistan and Tejikistan.

Oblivious to the heavy loss being sustained, Laden gave instructions to the terrorists to launch a new strike against the US interests according to the *Time Magazine*. In his pre-recorded message he said, "I swear to God that America will not live in peace before peace reigns in Palestine and before all the army of infidels depart the land of Muhammad". He defiantly praised the Sept, 11 hijack bombings saying, "a vanguard of Muslims" was behind the jet airliners attacks which razed the World Trade Center and damaged the Pentagon.

As the war progressed on the nineth day, the US military decided to target the Talibans brigade 55 an elite unit that includes Arab fighters loyal to Laden. The nineth day of raids with Jets streaking across the dawn sky over Kabul the US forces pounded targets around Kabul and attacked military head Quarters and a suspected training camp near the eastern city of Jalalabad.

Ironically the Deputy Prime Minister of the Taliban offered to surrender Laden for trial in an unspecified third country, if Washington stopped bombing and provided the Taliban with evidence of Laden's guilt. "We know he is guilty. "Turn him over', President Bush said in Washington.

The Special Forces of the U.S.swung into action on the tenth day raking a Taliban stronghold in Afghanistan with heavy machine guns devastating the Taliban jets at Kabul and wide airport complex at Kandahar which was holding about thirty housing units of Laden's followers.

President Bush declared on the eleventh day that the US led airstrikes have seriously weakened the Talibans defence paving the ground for a ground war. The US navy planes, flying from carriers stationed in the Indian Ocean also began patrolling specified "kill boxes" more precisely as "engagement zones".

After eleven days of non-stop bombing of Afghanistan and its Taliban troops the US special forces troop were on the ground in Afghanistan though President Bush declined to comment on the development of involving ground forces, "I will not comment on military operations" and reiterated, "we will do whatever is necessary to achieve our objective."

While addressing the twenty-one member Asia Pacific Economic Cooperation Summit at Shanghai on 20th October, President Bush urged the Asian leaders to join in his effort to end terrorism. President Bush with several Asian counter-parts made to them clear there was no isolation from evil in our world and our enemies are murderers with global reach and every nation now must oppose this enemy.

As the war progressed in favour of the US led forces more than 2000 US troops along with a large number of planes and helicopters descended over the three-air bases-Jacobabad. Pasni and Dalbandin provided by Pakistan. While the first two airports would act as logistical bases, the Dalibandin air base on the Afghanistan border was selected as forward operational base. The American forces used low flying aircraft and choppers for the first time to target terrorist bases in Afghanistan and to eliminate Laden and his Al-Qaeda network.

Informing the march of the US led forces, the US Secretary, Colin Powell said in Washington on 22nd October that the Alliance was likely soon to, "start moving on Kabul more aggressively and it would be in our interest and interest of the coalition to see this matter is resolved before winter strikes".

In an apparent move to help the Northern Alliance advance on major Afghan cities, the US jets pounded the Taliban postings near front lines outside the capital Kabul with an intention to gain on the ground before the winter sets in.

Eulogizing his fighters, the Taliban leader Mullah Mohammad Omar said after a fortnight of the war that his forces had benefited from divine intervention and promised eternal happiness to those killed in the fight against the US. The reclusive leader again called the Muslims all over the world to unite to Jehed (holy war) against the US and praised those killed. He further exhorted saying that if you can pursue Jehed with the sword, a tank or the pen, then this is the duty of all Muslims and they should fulfill this sacred obligation. Muslims inside and outside Afghanistan should know that death in this sacred way is martyrdom and will ensure eternal happiness".

Unable to bear the severe pressure from the US air strikes and opposition ground attacks the Taliban accused the US of deploying chemical and biological weapons to flush out Laden. The US quickly denied the allegation.

With barely three weeks left for the start of the Muslim holy month of Ramzan the US intensified its blitz against the Taliban in Afghanistan on 23rd October, launching a three pronged assault on the key city of Mazar-e-Sharif front line positions and targets in and around the capital Kabul. The US jets also pounded front line troops in the Northern Afghanistan and dropped bombs north of Kabul where the Taliban troops have been entrenched.

The US virtually rejected Pakistan President Musharaf's plea for a halt in the US led attacks against Afghanistan while agreeing to the fact that one must be respectful of the Muslim holy month but at the same time the US "mission" in Afghanistan must continue. The Secretary of Defence, Donald Rumsfeld further asserted that history was replete with instances where Muslim nations have fought among themselves or with other countries on important holy days of their religion.

On the seventeenth day of fight against the Taliban ruled Afghanistan, the US navy fighter Jets accidentally dropped 1000 pound bomb near a senior citizens' home in the Northern Afghan city of Herat and two 500 pound bombs in a residential area north west of Kabul which resulted in civilian causalities

US Defence Secretary, Donald Rumsfled has admitted after eighteen days of war against Taliban led Afghanistan that the American forces might not catch Laden but asserted that "the Taliban regime will be toppled and that was easier than finding a single person".

In a jolt to President Musharaf, the U.S. has said that Pakistan cannot again" "foist a government of its choice" in post Taliban Afghanistan and ruled out the possibility of any pause in its military action against Afghanistan during the festival month of Ramzan.

As some 70 Christians gathered for the Sunday morning services on the 28th of October, six masked men on three motor cycles rode upto Saint Dominic's Church Bahawalpur, Pakistan and pulled AK-47 assault rifles out of their bags and shouting, "Graveyard of Christians, Pakistan and Afghanistan and this is just a start" raced upto the Church while the guards were asleep and opened fire killing eighteen of them. Women wailing over the bodies of Christians lying in pools of blood cried, "we have nothing to do what is going on in Afghanistan. We are innocent people and not supporting the attacks in Afghanistan"

On the next day the Pakistan police have arrested eleven people suspected to have got connection with Sunday's carnage. The Americans were suspecting that Pakistan has atleast 24 nuclear warheads that can be delivered by intermediate-range missiles and F-16 airplanes. The US regional experts doubted President Musharaf's ability to control the military and Pakistan's nuclear arsenal if there was a coup-and said that the dissident fundamentalists within the military might try to seize a nuclear warhead.

One day before the end of October, the U.S. planes targeted suspected underground command centres of Laden and his Al-Qaeda network and also the Taliban stronghold of Kandhar while the Northern Alliance forces have mobilised hundreds of elite fighters near the frontline north of Kabul. The cities of Jalalabad, Mazar-e-Sharif and the capital city of Kabul were also targeted and there were indications that the American ground forces would soon be deployed to establish a base in Afghanistan.

Veteran war correspondent, Tony Clifton who covered several American military engagements from Vietnam to Iraq predicted that the Americans will be in Afghanistan for years, if they don't change their war tactics. He suggested to send agents with tens of millions of dollars to buy the cave where Laden was hiding and pay the Taliban to defect.

The American public wants a quick end to the country's involvement and the US must move fast to keep its coalition intact. On the other hand the Taliban's strategy was to hold out for the next few weeks until Ramadan, sit out the winter, when the Americans send in ground troops to drag them through the streets" and wait for the will of the U.S. to crumble.

The Americans who were shrugging off new terror thrilled to see President Bush travelling to a packed and patriotic Yankee stadium to open the third game of baseball's world series with a perfect strike. He urged the Americans to go about business as usual, to take vacations, to fly again and to go to ball parks all the while remaining alert.

Some U.S. officials were suspecting that Pakistan is covertly sending military supplies and other goods to the Taliban militia despite President Musharaff's support to the U.S. led military compaign. The trade was approved by officials of the Pakistan military and the ISI, which takes place at night by trucks. The ISI in particular was said to still have close ties with the Taliban regime even though there were changes in its leadership carried out by President Musharaff.

The Northern Alliance in Afghanistan are traditionally friends of India. As such, India has been supplying both money and material to the North Alliance. After the terror attacks the U.S. has created a task force to check the members or supporters of 46 out-fits designated by it as "terrorist organisations" from entering the country and those who were already inside deported.

By the end of October the U.S. led air compaign entered the 26th day with Washington warning the Taliban regime to brace more carpet-bombing of their positions across the country. Atleast one B-52 bomber was spotted dropping large numbers of unguided bombs over the Taliban frontlines north of Kabul. The U.S. bombs severely damaged Afghanistan's biggest dam and power station cutting electricity to two major cities.

Facing the U.S. led forces boldly the Taliban captured supporters of a top aide to the exiled former king, Mohammad Zahir Shah who was on an under-cover mission in Afghanistan. The militia captured 25 followers of the former Afghan deputy foreign minister, Hamid Karzai in confrontation in Deharwad in Uruzgan province.

While the war was going interminably in Afghanistan, Laden the prime suspect surfaced via video on the third October criticizing the U.N. as an "instrument of crimes" and referred to Kashmir where he said our brethren" had been slaughtered for fifty years. Laden was still challenging the U.S. to produce proof of his involvement in terror attacks on New York and Washington cities.

Even after more than thirty days of bombing the U.S. could not lay its hands on Laden. When they found that the Northern Alliance locked in fierce battle with the Taliban the U.S. moved more forces into Afghanistan to help the Northern Alliance to capture Mazar-e-Sharif and then jets dropped bombs on the Taliban's stronghold of Kandahar and near Mazar-e-Sharif.

As the war was in progress with heavy bombing of important cities of Afghanistan the U.S. has also taken strong measures to protect President Musharaff from, removal and also the Pakistan's nuclear weapons falling into the hands of fundamentalists or Laden. In case if President Musharaff was overthrown by the forces friendly to Laden the 2,200 troops of the 15th marine expeditionary cooped up on the assault ship the *USS Peleliu*, ready for action could be sent to safeguard the Pakistan nuclear weapons and materials to keep away from Laden or other terrorists.

Mullah Abdul Salam Zaeef, the Taliban Ambassador to Pakistan turned to be a big draw for the international media present in Pakistan to cover the war in Afghanistan has been banned by Pakistan from holding daily media briefings highlighting the Taliban propaganda against the U.S. military operations in Afghanistan.

The month long U.S. led air strikes against Afghanistan have destroyed the Taliban's air defence, disrupted their communications and lines of command and reduced their military hardware. However, Laden continues to taunt the Americans from his secret hideouts while his friend and ally Omar was still the undisputed leader of most of the country.

The British Prime Minister, Tony Blair was another important world leader who criss- crossed the globe to convince the leaders of other countries and cement support to America's war on terorism and to defeat Laden and Afghanistan's Taliban regime. He said "I have a huge respect for President Bush describing him as "very focussed, very determined and someone who genuinely involves other people. But takes the decisions and taken them well." He supported Bush to continue air strikes on the Taliban targets during the Muslims, holy month of Ramadan as the Taliban will not stop during Ramadan neither will Bin Laden".

As the situation in the War-torned Afghanistan has become from bad to worst the rift between the Pakistan and the Taliban ruled Afghanistan has also widened. The Pakistan therefore asked Afghanistan's Taliban regime to close its consulate in the Southern Pakistani Port City of Karachi.

In order to strengthen the U.S. military forces, the Pentagon has despatched a fourth aircraft carrier "*Battle Group*" to waters near Afghanistan. The *Battle Group* was led by the San Diego-based carrier *USS Stennis*.

Abdul Saleem Zaeef, the Ambassador to Islamabad who was asked by Pakistan not to hold press conferences reacted sharply and asked Pakistan to tell the U.S. missions to stop using "foul language" against Afghanistan. He again reasserted that the Taliban would never hand over Laden. "We will fight for one hundred years but Afghans will not abandon Islam" he said. He further told the news paper editors that "how could we violate Islamic principles and hand over Laden without any proof".

On one hand, the Ambassador to Islamabad was boosting that Afghans will fight for hundred years and on the other President Musharaff is pitting the Taliban controlled Afghanistan saying that this war was against the poor, miserable and innocent people and asked President Bush to suspend the bombings during Ramadan which starts in mid-November. However rejecting a call from the President of Pakistan to halt military operations in Afghanistan during Ramadan the U.S. officials have said that the defeat of the Taliban is essential to relieving the sufferings of Afghanistan populace.

Considering the food drops by the U.S. as an "insult" to the Afghan people the Taliban controlled radio station issued warnings to people that food rations dropped by the U.S. aircraft could be poisoned. Continuous bombing of the U.S led forces in the cities of Taliban controlled Afghanistan has not affected the four teenaged sons; Hamza, Mohammad, Khaleed and Laden of Osama Bin Laden. One of the sons praised Omar as symbol of manhood and pride.

Once the elephants were used in the battle and dolphins for protecting submarines. Now the North Alliance is using 2000 horses to attack the Taliban Tanks in Afghanistan.

After a month of war against Afghanistan the opposition forces of the Taliban entered Mazar-e-Sharif and took control over the key northern city. Terrified to face the mighty US force in Afghanistan the supporters of the Taliban issued a threat to Nepal that it has planned to hijack an aircraft from the kingdom of Nepal and slam them into residence or office of the Indian Prime Minister and the U.S. embassy in New Delhi.

A question was persistently posed to the U.S. officials as why the U.S. was counselling restraint to India when it suffers terrorism and lost the lives of about 70,000 people but when terrorism hits America it went half way across the world to go into war against Afghanistan. Though they could not give any satisfactory explanation, they however, realized that terrorism should be rejected in all its forms. After the first summit meeting with the Prime Minister Atal Behari Vajpayee, in Washington on the 9th November, President Bush declared that terrorism must be rejected in all its forms and "murder in all its guises".

The American aircraft dropped atleast seven bombs on different locations including a village in the Qarabagh and Istateef districts to the north of Kabul and killed twenty eight Afghans. In yet another development a U.S. warplane has killed thirteen Saudi Arabians in a raid on the Taliban positions in Afghanistan.

The Taliban acknowledged after a month of fierce fighting that they lost the key city of Mazar-e-Sharif to the Northern Alliance. However, the U.S. jets were searching for Taliban units to attack them from the air.

After banning several militant organizations in Britain, the British Government took emergency powers permitting the indefinite detention of foreigners, suspected of terrorism in order to tighten security after the September 11 attacks.

The support of Pakistan to the U.S. led forces against the Taliban ruled Afghanistan was not received well inspite of several statements issued by President Musharaf that he supported the U.S. for the benefit of Pakistan and Kashmir. Several pro-Taliban protests took in Pakistan since that day and many were killed when the Pakistan police opened fire on them.

Fear has also gripped of possible strikes against the Pakistan's nuclear facilities and its nuclear devices and missile material could be vulnerable to attack or theft. President Musharaf, therefore, ordered an emergency re-deployment of the nuclear arsenal to atleast six new locations and reorganized military oversight of the nuclear forces. Pakistan has got required materials to assemble between thirty and forty nuclear warheads.

Backed by the U.S. bombers and firing relentless volleys of heavy artillery, the Northern Alliance fighters engaged the Taliban frontline some 25km north of Kabul for the first time since raids began thirty-seven days back. The roar of rocket fire, artillery and mortars filled the air as the Alliance forces fired on the Taliban positions just hours after they came under blistering fire from the US F 18 and B52 planes from the air.

Even after heavy bombing by the US led air-strikes Omar and Laden are safe and sound and Omar was directing the Taliban forces in different directions.

22

KABUL FALLS TO THE NORTHERN ALLIANCE

After the thirty-eight days of fierce battle, Kabul was taken over by the Northern Alliance forces aided by the American pounding from the sky. The Northern Alliance forces defying international pressure, especially the US, to stay away marched into the ravaged city of Kabul, meeting little or no resistance, welcomed by cheering residents. The Taliban soldiers plundered Afghanistan's main currency market before fleeing in the night in a convoy of Tanks armoured personnel carriers and battered pick up trucks heading for their stronghold in Kandahar. They took with them eight western aid-workers (two Americans, two Australians and four Germans) facing charges of promoting Christianity. Soon after the news came out that the Taliban fled for fear of the Northern Alliance onward march many people with their small transistors flooded the city with rejoicement. Under the Taliban rule all men were mandated to wear a beard following their strict interpretation of Islam. Following the retreat of the Taliban many Afghan found shaving their beards.

The end game in the war to topple, the Taliban appeared to be certain across Southern Afghanistan on the fifteenth of November 2001 as the US special forces launched a hunt on the ground for Laden and the Taliban protectors tried to hold on to their southern base of Kandahar and vowed to fight to the death. Pakistan moved troops and tanks to southwest border with Afghanistan in a swift response to reports that Laden could try to sneak across the border.

In Kunduz several Taliban fighters were also resisting troops of the Northern Alliance who had surrounded them. Many were reported to be Laden's Arab followers who feared they would be killed if they surrendered to their Afghan foes. There were 20,000 Talibans in Kunduz many of them Arabs and they were trying to break out.

A defiant Taliban supremo Omar warned on 14th November of a big plan to destroy the US within a short period of time and refused to join a broad based Government in Afghanistan. In an interview to BBC radio's Pashto language service over satellite phone he said, "we will not accept a Government of wrong doers. We prepared death than to be a part of an evil Government" and added that the current situation in Afghanistan is related to a bigger cause, that is the destruction of America. "If God help is with us this will happen within a short period of time. Keep it in mind this prediction," he said. The set-backs suffered by the Taliban was not worrying Omar. He said," it makes no difference if we control one or two or twenty provinces" once we did not even have a single province but later we captured all the provinces.

Ignoring appeals form the Islamic world to cease bombing Afghanistan in the holy month of Ramzan which began on the 16th November, the US war planes pounded the Taliban bastion of Kandahar destroying the militia's foreign ministry building and a mosque. Under relentless onslaught from the U.S. war planes raining bombs and troops of anti-Taliban tribal groups, the Taliban supremo, Omar has agreed to leave his bastion Kandahar within 24 hours and handover the city to non-Taliban Pasthun leaders and took decision to leave Khandhar and retreat into the mountains.

Experts in the U.S. government are taking Laden's nuclear threat seriously and on a high state of alert for 24 hours a day and seven days a week. They suspect that Laden instead of building an ordinary nuclear bomb could have obtained nuclear related materials that could be dispersed by exploding a conventional bomb.

President Bush, who was very pleased with the progress in the war, however, warned it would be dangerous to assume that the Taliban had collapsed and reminded the need for destruction of Laden's network.

In an attack on the Taliban led Afghanistan by the forces of the Northern Alliance forces well supported by the U.S. led air forces, the Al-Qaeda leader and lieutenant to Laden, Mohammad Atef died creating a big gap in the Taliban forces. The U.S. special forces on ground in Afghanistan persistently engaged in combat and eliminating the Taliban forces. Though no U.S. troops have died according to the U.S Defence Secretary they had, however faced difficult situations on occasions during combat in the middle of November in driving the Taliban from Mazar-I-Sharif in the North.

Without any respite, despite the beginning of Ramadan the U.S. war planes pounded militia portions in Kunduz and Kandahar. The home of a key Taliban Commander, Jalaluddin Haquani and a seminary were bombed near the eastern town of Khost.

Frightened to fight the US led forces the Taliban forces approached the U.N. to negotiate the surrender. The U.N. has rejected the request of the Taliban to negotiate the surrender of over 20,000 fighters mostly Arabs and Pakistanis surrounded by the Northern Alliance force, as its advice was not heeded by the Taliban previously.

The Taliban forces hold up in the besieged Northern town of Kunduz offered on 19th November conditional surrender even as the U.S. war planes continued to rain bombs on the Taliban front lines in north-east and south of Afghanistan amid intensive efforts to set up an interim government in the country.

The U.S. authorities firmly believed that Laden, world's most wanted man in Afghanistan, will be caught. As more and more of the country was released from the Taliban control he had fewer and fewer places in which to hide said the Secretary of State. Colin

Powell. The U.S. and Pakistan were working closely together to prevent Laden from escaping from Afghanistan.

The spread of the Al-Qaeda network in China was already pricking the Chinese Government. The Government has, therefore decided to adopt a comprehensive approach to stamp out foreign and domestic hostile forces and cult groups to improve public security.

The U.S. based analysts on geo-politics predict that the Taliban may wage guerilla war soon. They say that the Talibans withdrawal from major Afghan cities was simply an abandonment of frontal warfare to use guerilla tactics that was more suited to their numbers and resources.

Several hundred Taliban fighters have surrendered in the area around Kunduz as the Northern Alliance pressed its drive against the besieged bastion of the Islamic militia. The Taliban forces were dislodged from hillside position around the city of Khanabad near Kunduz.

It was claimed that the Taliban troops defending their strong hold of Kandahar might have five hundred tanks and would defend the ancient city to their last breath. Mullah Bismillah in charge of the Taliban ammunition depot claimed that they have all kinds of weapons and ammunition to defend themselves. If there was a ground attack by America they will fight to their last breath.

Apprehensive of the rain of bombs, eight hundred Taliban fighters had surrendered east of Kunduz fighting with their eight tanks five anti-air-craft guns, two bm22 rocket launchers and five smaller bm12 rocket launchers as well as sixty vehicles. Many of the estimated fifteen thousand fighters under siege in Kunduz were believed to be Pakistani, Arabs and Chechen fighters loyal to Laden and his Al-Qaeda network and getting them to lay down their weapons was no easy task.

On the other hand in the last week of November the US launched attack on the Taliban and number of terrorists in Southern Afghanistan backed by helicopter gunships. But the US special forces commandos reported to have come under heavy firing by the Taliban as soon as the helicopter dropped them. The US troops were caught by surprise and the attack form the Taliban forces was so intense that the special forces had to quickly withdraw without any operational achievement. Thirtyfive US commandos reported to have been killed and this was one of the heaviest causalities suffered by the US army since they launched attacks against the Taliban on the seventh October,2001.

The prisoners numbering about four hundred to five hundred, who had surrendered from the besieged city of Kunduz staged a violent uprising. Number of prisoners who revolted were Pakistanis, Arabs and Chechen and they disarmed their guards after killing a senior alliance commander with a hand grenade. A vicious gun battle took place in the prison and about one hundred were killed, Mr.Spann, a CIA Officer of America was also killed during the upraising.

President Bush warned Americans that the US war on terrorism was far form over. Unable to bear the incessant bombing by the US led forces over one thousand, Taliban fighters surrendered in Kunduz by the last week of November. One Taliban fighter who surrendered himself told that the "foreigners have taken decision to fight". They will not surrender. As the US led war to punish the Taliban for protecting Laden was entered its eighth week, Bush cautioned that the fight against terrorism might be prolonged. We will face difficult times ahead" , Bush said in his weekly radio address to Americans celebrating thanks giving.

While the war is going on in the frontier of Afghanistan, majority of the Britains believe that Muslims who support Laden should be deported. About five hundred US marines have taken an air strip in southern Afghanistan the first major seizing of Afghan territory by American governed forces. This would be decisive battle for the capture of the Taliban's last remaining stronghold of Kandahar as nearly four hundred Taliban rebels who staged a bloody upraising in a jail were killed by the American backed North Alliance. The Alliance forces took complete control of the Northern city of Kunduz after a fierce battle with the diehard Taliban militia.

The landing of the US marines in Kandahar means the Americans were willing to take a huge risk. They had sofar confined themselves of making the passage smoother for the Northern Alliance by bombing and destroying vital installations of the Taliban and the Al-Qaeda. The fall of one city after another to the Northern Alliance showed the US strategy as having met with success. The US also wished to show to the world that it was not afraid of a ground war also. The deployment of the marines could also be a measure of the US confidence not only about their invincibility but their abilities in locating Laden.

There was an imperative need for the US to complete the present operation against the Taliban atleast by mid December. Geographically, Afghanistan is a land locked country packed with rugged mountains. It is also the site of some of the most extreme weather conditions in South-West Asia particularly during the winter season. The country is atleast three hundred miles away from the ocean and the average elevation of the Hindu Kush ranges which cover the north western and north eastern parts of the country is in the region of 5000 feet. In the South West lie the Marco deserts. Both Kabul and Mazar-e-Sharif receive snow fall for about a week in a month and it would become extremely difficult to identify military targets.

In eastern Afghanistan the U.S. led forces destroyed a village and killed between one hundred to two hundred civilians at the beginning of December month. Kandahar the Taliban's last stronghold had not been encircled by the anti-Taliban forces and was still firmly under the control of the Islamic militia. More than one thousand U.S. marines who were stationed at a desert base about one hundred and ten kilo meters (110 Km) South West of Kandahar did not take part in the fighting for Kandahar.

The senior officials of Pakistan military regime have admitted that as many as eight thousand Pakistani citizens who went to Afghanistan to fight along with the Taliban militia were either dead or missing which caused a lot of discomfort to President Musharaf. Added to this, the U.S. air strikes killed one hundred civilians and wounded nearly two hundred in Jalalabad and the Taliban still claiming that Kandahar air port was under their control.

Laden's Al-Qaeda net-work has shifted twenty Russian made oragan missiles to Tora Bora mountain base in Afghanistan to use them against the U.S.led forces. However the U.S. forces continued their bombings into the cave riddled mountains of Tora Bora in eastern Afghanistan where Laden suspected to be hiding.

Kandahar was one of the Taliban strong holds and therefore the U.S. fighter jets circled over Southern Kandahar at the end of sixty days War. The U.S. marines have joined the Northern Alliance forces in laying siege to Kandahar in their first offensive operation since seizing a desert airfield South of the Taliban capital in the last week of November.

Unable to fight the mighty U.S. led forces, Omar agreed after two months of war to surrender Kandahar the only city under his control. Afghan interim leader Hamid Karzai who negotiated the surrender with the Taliban representatives made it clear that he had offered general amnesty to the "Common Taliban: but Omar would not be granted amnesty till he renounces terrorism.

After two months of fierce fighting the Taliban have surrendered Kandahar, their final bastion and birthplace. The Anti-Taliban forces confirmed, they had also seized mountain hideout but had failed to trace Laden. Though the U.S. led coalition rejoiced at the fall of Kandahar, they however vowed to pursue the war until it met its goals of crushing the Taliban and Laden's Al-Qaeda net-work and bring their leaders to justice. However, there was no trace of Laden and Omar in the besieged Kandahar and it was suspected that they might have slipped away from the area.

For the Taliban history has come full circle, Kandahar which was once a launching pad has become a graveyard for them. The Taliban rule is finished after Hamid Karzai took over as new chief of the interim administration in Afghanistan in the first week of December. The future of Laden and Omar is shrouded in mystery as both have slipped away from the scene of war and clandestinely hiding in an unknown place. After attaining power in Kabul both these fanatic individuals tried and to some extent succeeded to reflect an attitude and ideology that was perverse, obscuranist and fundamentalist. They incited the Americans by attacking the World Trade Center, and the Pentagon and in retaliation when the U.S. led forces rained innumerable bombs setting ablaze the important cities of Afghanistan they pushed the Taliban forces in the hungry mouths of American and other forces and fled from the War ravaged scene with their families.

Shelling and heavy machine gunfire echoed across the valleys in Tora Bora as B-52 S and the U.S. surveillance aircraft circled above. With the help of the U.S. war planes pounding the mountainous area the tribal fighters were successful in capturing lot of caves where hundreds of the Al-Qaeda fighters had made a stand. Unable to fight against the tribal fighters some retreating Al-Qaeda workers were willing to discuss surrender terms after losing key Mountain in fierce fighting.

Deadly Daisy Cutter bombs and robotic spy planes designed for the cold war were used by the U.S. successfully in Afghanistan to kill the Al-Qaeda fighters. The U.S. has also engaged two new spy planes, the unmanned *Global Hawk* and the four-engine *JSTARS surveillance* in Afghanistan.

After a fresh dead line for the surrender of the Al-Qaeda fighters expired the U.S. planes blasted eastern Afghan mountain hideouts of Laden and his fighters. What could be assumed as a final stage of the battle the U.S. led forces bombed cave and valley hideouts of Laden's Al-Qaeda net-work and possibly of Laden itself. As the net closed around Laden, hundreds of heavily armed U.S. Marines swept into Kandahar Airport in the heart of the southern power base of the ousted Taliban protectors to secure the airfield and its facilities.

With Laden eluding the U.S. military might even by the middle of December the U.S. war planes carried out some of their most intensive bombing raids on the caves and tunnels burrowed in eastern

Afghanistan's Tora Bora mountains. In an effort to destroy a final area of fierce resistance by followers of Laden, the U.S. even unleashed the most powerful, the 15,000 lb. (6,800 kg) Daisy Cutter also.

Hundreds of the Al-Qaeda fighters have battled to death in a last stand in eastern Afghanistan but their leader Laden was still eluding the U.S. dragnet. Huge U.S. B-2- bombers pierced through the skies on the first day of Ramdan dropping huge bombs on suspected Al-Qaeda positions through the night and the morning. The U.S. Defence Secretary, Donald Rumsfeld was the first Senior American official to visit near Kabul on 16th December after the U.S. forces toppled the Taliban from power. In their quest for Laden and his fighters the U.S. forces have found some important materials and documents at a former Al-Qaeda guerilla base.

The U.S. and Afghan forces were in hot pursuit of Laden after flushing his Al-Qaeda fighters out of their bastion in Tora Bora. The whereabouts of Laden still surrounded in mystery, his options to cross to the neighboring Pakistan was diminishing as Pakistani forces were intensely patrolling the Afghan border to prevent him and his forces. On the other side, the Afghan forces were preparing to attack a mountainous region north-west of Kandahar where they believed Omar was hiding with five hundred men.

After the fall of Tora Bora to the fighters of the Northern Alliance scores of the Al-Qaeda forces were hiding in Islamic Seminaries and refugee camps in Pakistan after fleeing from Afghanistan with a view to reorganise and launch a fresh wave of Anti-American Campaign. There were, however, unconfirmed reports that Laden might have slipped past Pakistan Border patrols when hundreds of his loyalists on the run near the border of Pakistan. Pakistan border patrols had arrested number of the Al-Qaeda fighters fleeing the Tora Bora mountains to escape from the onslaught of the U.S. led forces.

U.S. officials have interrogated prisoners, scrutinised surveillance photos and asked for help from friendly forces to track down the top Taliban and the Al-Qaeda leaders who have disappeared in Afghanistan. The U.S. helped the Anti-Taliban Afghans to clear caves one by one in the Tora Bora areas, the last bastion of the Al-Qaeda who hurriedly abandoned the caves leaving ammunition, guns, surface to air missiles and other weapons.

As the new interim Government with Hamid Karzai as Prime Minister was ready to take over the reigns of Afghanistan after the Taliban Government, the U.S. agents interrogated around seven thousand fighters of the Al-Qaeda network for clues as to the whereabouts of Laden. Captured prisoners were screened to ascertain also whether they were merely sympathisers and "late comers" to the Taliban and the Al-Qaeda or hard-liners.

After heavy bombing in strategic areas of Afghanistan the U.S. troops have begun searching the Al-Qaeda caves and tunnels in Afghanistan and more U.S. led forces were pressed into service to hunt for guerrillas and intelligence in the dangerous mountains. Ground searches have replaced heavy bombing in the eleven week war on terrorism in battle-scarred Afghanistan. British government had also deployed in the Afghan capital for the first time on 22nd December 2001 twenty commandos for assisting the security at the interior ministry.

U.S.President George Bush poured scorn on Laden and made it clear that the Afghan calls for a quick end to the U.S. bombing would not be met until the U.S. found Laden dead or alive. Bush also urged the Americans to remain on the alert in case of new attacks by Laden's Al-Qaeda network saying he had intelligence report that the group blamed for September,11 suicide hijack attack was bent on more destruction.

The U.S. bombers and attack planes have struck a military compound in eastern Afghanistan where members of Laden's terrorist network were regrouping. It was the first American air strike in Afghanistan since 28th, December and reflected the U.S. military's concern that remnants of the Al-Qaeda network were trying to reorganize as the search for Laden continued by air, land and sea.

The U.S. was determined to pursue Laden and his top lieutenants as well as Omar and the other Taliban leaders for as long as it takes to capture or kill them.

However, fighting was under way in the East where the U.S. forces believed units of the Al-Qaeda were regrouping. Amid fears, the Al-Qaeda fighters might have taken shelter in surrounding hills after fleeing nearby Tora Bora region, the U.S. bombers pounded hills near the eastern Afghanistan city of Jalalabad to flush out the suspected Al-Qaeda fighters holed up there.

The U.S. jets prowled the skies overhead, bombing parts of Paktia Province where Laden once ran, training camps and where he or his Al-Qaeda fighters might have taken refuge. The U.S. helicopters also landed in the area near the Zawara training camp delivering the U.S. ground troops for search operation for remnants of the Al-Qaeda and the vanquished Taliban militia.

The U.S. believed that the hardline Al-Qaeda guerillas were trying to regroup in eastern Afghanistan where the U.S. warplanes again bombed a battered training camp when tanks emerged from caves. The aircraft attacked a cave complex at Zhawar Kili near Tora Bora, where the Al-Qaeda guerrillas tried to regroup.

For the fifth time in a week the U.S. war planes bombed an Al-Qaeda cave complex in eastern Afghanistan even as an American military refuelling aircraft with seven marines on board crashed in flames into a mountain in south-western Pakistan on ninth January. The U.S. bombers again struck the Zhawar Kili base where the Al-Qaeda and the Taliban fighters tried to regroup destroying several buildings. Two senior Al-Qaeda fighters were among a group of guerrillas captured by the US forces near the vast underground cave complex at Zhawar kili.

The U.S. sent the first group of prisoners captured in Afghanistan to newly prepared detention facilities at a naval base at Quantanamo Bay, Cuba amid debate about the fate of many of the detainees.

The U.S. War planes resumed intense bombing on the 12th

January,2002 of suspected Al-Qaeda hideouts in Zhawar district in eastern Afghanistan. Zhawar is about five kilometers from the Pakistan border. The American fighter jets used explosive devices of high intensity in their new onslaught on the Zawahar area in Khost Province. The U.S. commandos conducted ground operations in Zhawar, former guerilla bases and training camps run by the former Taliban Minister Moulvi Jalaluddin Haqqani to flush out members of the Al-Qaeda terrorist network headed by Laden.

Florida police cast doubt on a confidential informant's claim that the Middle Easterners planned to kill Governor Jeb.Bush the younger brother of President George W.Bush with a truck bomb, to avenge the killing of several Al-Qaeda fighters and bombing of number of places in Afghanistan by the U.S. military forces.

A video tape found in a house in Afghanistan associated with the Al-Qaeda helped the Singapore authorities to capture the alleged members of a terrorist cell planning to blow up Western embassies, the U.S. naval vessels and a bus that transports American military service members. The official disclosure of Singapore Government marks the first time a foreign Government has publicly acknowledged that evidence found by the U.S. forces in Afghanistan was used to thwart a planned terrorist operation in its territory.

The videotape released on 13th January 2002 allegedly showed Laden's Al-Qaeda network training terrorists for a mass assassination of world leaders at a golf tournament. The U.S. launched some of its fiercest raids yet seen on areas around eastern Khost where the Al-Qaeda fighters were believed to have regrouped in caves after weeks of defeats. But while Laden remained elusive another longtime American foe Iraqi leader Saddam Hussain was in the sights of the Bush administration.

The extensive Al-Qaeda training complex that the U.S. warplanes have been bombing since 3rd January, 2002 was one of the dozens in dry cave-riddled valleys of South Eastern Afghanistan where groups of terrorist fighters suspected to be hiding. This entire part of Afghanistan is riddled with hillsides and valleys of caves and above ground structures. Therefore, there were likely other valleys and they in fact may very well have the Al-Qaeda militants.

Air strikes on Zawar Kili were tapering off. Over the weekend of January 2002, B-52 and B-1 bombers and F/A-18 navy jet fighters pummeled bombs using precision bombs to blow up entrances and level buildings in an area of more than three square miles. On 13th January the bombing of the U.S. on the cave complex of Tora Bora appeared to be heaviest.

The Al-Qaeda and Taliban prisoners were shaved for health reasons before being transferred to the U.S. base at Guantanamo Bay, Cuba denying any violation of Islamic law. As a matter of fact there is no requirement in the Muslim religion to have a beard. All of the Muslim prisoners had been offered a copy of the Koran, a second towel for prayers.

The U.S. forces searched cave complexes and bunkers in eastern Afghanistan to find information that, the U.S. officials believed to be useful to thwart further terrorist attacks by the Al-Qaeda network. The U.S. personnel were already in possession of computers, hard drives and diaries as well as several filing cabinets full of documentary evidence that were taken out in the process of going through very methodically.

A U.S. military helicopter with seven marines on board crashed on 12th January 2002 in high mountain terrain in northern Afghanistan. Two of the marines were confirmed dead while five were injured.

In the most intense fighting in the month of January, 2002 Americans killed as many as fifteen Taliban fighters and captured twenty-seven others in a pre-dawn on the 25th January, sixty miles north of Khandar. The raid conducted by the Army Special forces supported byAC-130 gunships could indicate the escalation in attacks on mountain hideouts north of Kandahar, the Taliban's political and spiritual capital.

U.S. Secretary of Defenoe, Rumsfeld said on 3rd Feb. that Iran had aided Islamic militants escaping across the Afghanistan border. He said that the U.S. has got number of reports that Iran had been permissive and allowed transit through their country to the Al-Qaeda.

President Bush decided on 7th Feb. that the Geneva Convention would be applied to the Taliban captives being held in Cuba but not to the Al-Qaeda detainees. The Bush Administration had already decided not to grant prisoner of war status to any of the captives. The denial of prisoner of war status means that the U.S. need not have to repatriate the captives promptly to their countries at the end of the war.

The man who served the Taliban as Foreign Minister surrendered to the new Afghan authorities in Kandahar on 8th February 2002 and was transferred to American custody. As Foreign Minister Mullah Muttavakil held secret discussions with Pakistan officials about handing over of Laden to the Americans. Thirty years old Mullah Muttavakil attended a religious school in Quetta, Pakistan.

An elusive 30 years old Palestinian who travelled the world using false passports and multiple aliases has emerged as the new chief of operations for the Al-Qaeda believed to be organising remnants of the terrorist network to carry out new attacks against the U.S. The Palestinian Abu Zubaydah has been linked directly to the planning of the September, 11 strikes in the U.S. The American investigators said that they were convinced that Zubaydah was trying to activate the Al-Qaeda sleeper cells for new strikes in the U.S. and in the countries of its allies. He is as dangerous as any one for whom they were looking for including Laden.

Ayman al Zawahri, the right hand man of Laden was arrested after a long pursuit and imprisoned in the Iranian Capital's *Evin Prison*. An Afghan force backed by ageing armour and modern war planes advanced to the foot of the Al-Qaeda and the Taliban mountain fortification and prepared for an assault that commanders hoped finally wipe out the guerrilla holdouts burrowed inside. While the U.S. planes bombed enemy positions, tanks and troop trucks rumbled down dirty roads and across a desert expanse to take up positions at Shahikot. Advance teams clambered up nearby peaks to seize strategic heights. Atleast 1,150 Afghan reinforcements linked up with 1800 U.S. and Afghan troops that have been trading fire with the guerrillas from the first week of March, 2002.

The *Operation Anaconda* which began on March, 2002 involving more than one thousand U.S. ground troops and almost one thousand Afghans ended on the 19th of March. However, the U.S. troops continued to kill or capture the Al-Qaeda fighters throughout Afghanistan.

The Americans with the support of allied forces thus have driven out the Taliban from Kabul and in its place a new more broad based Government has been established. In the war the Al-Qaeda's training camps and organizational infrastructures have been smashed and its leaders are on the run.

Financially also Washington claimed a large measure of success in blocking terrorist funds. The U.S. Attorney General, Ashcroft, said that more than 100 million dollars have been frozen in the U.S. plus perhaps half that abroad.

Whatever the success, the U.S. has made militarily and financially blocking the terrorist funds, they have not forgotten the scars of September 11 attacks.on Newyork and Washington. Life came to standstill across the U.S. on September, 11 2002, one year after the two terrorist flown air crafts pierced through the twin towers of World Trade Center, killing over 2800 people that compelled a new global onslaught on terrorism.

As the day broke over Manhattan in the *Big Apple* rest of the U.S. and across the World a sombre memorial service began at *Ground Zero* where once the two majestic towers were giving pride to the Americans. As an emotionally overcome kin of those killed in the attacks stood near *Ground Zero* with photographs of their beloved ones. Governor George Palaki read Abraham Lincoln's famous *Gettysbug Address* against injustice.

In Washington, President Bush joined the Defense Secretary, Donal Rumsfeld observed a minute's silence and prayer at a ceremony on the White House Lawns. Renewing the U.S. commitment to win the War that began on September, 11 2001 Bush said "the murder of innocents cannot' be explained, only endured".

23

NEW GOVERNMENT OF AFGHANISTAN

After crushing defeat of the Tliban Government in Afghanistan a regime change in Afghanistan has constituted the next political phase of the campaign against terrorism. A stable internationally supported Government was necessary to carry on the Government bereft of religious fanatics. It was a terrible event to foresee what would happen after the collapse of the Taliban followed by a power vaccum in Kabul.

While the war was going on in Afghanistan the Northern Alliance with the help of the U.S. led airstrikes captured many important cities and vowed to wipe off the entire Taliban Government from Afghanistan. When the Taliban led Government was out, it was necessary to fill the vaccum immediately. Therefore, six nations viz., China, Iran, Pakistan, Tajikistan, Turkmenistan and Uzbekistan bordering Afghanistan plus Russia and the U.S. who were called 6+2 have passed a declaration on the 13th November, 2001 saying a "broad basis multi-ethnic politically balanced, freely chosen Government should assume power in Kabul". The Foreign Ministers of the above countries urged the United Nations to work urgently to help Afghan groups establish such an administration.

Amidst conflicting reports of the Taliban withdrawal from their stronghold of Kandahar, the former exiled Afghanistan President

Burhanuddin Rabbani arrived in Kabul on 17th November even as the U.S. war planes showing no pause despite the beginning of Ramadan and attacked militia positions in Kunduz and Kandahar. Rabbani was forced out of Kabul by the Taliban in 1996 but has remained as the United Nations recognized Head of State. The U.N. has held out against granting Rabbani any special status and was trying to set up talks outside Afghanistan. Although, the U.N. and majority of countries still recognize Rabbani as the Country's President, many Afghan groups rejected his authority.

The United Nations was also backing the ex-king, Mohammad Zahir Shah who lives in exile in Rome as a possible leader of a transitional Government that could unite all of Afghanistan's rival factions.

Delighted with the defeat of the Taliban day by day a fresh sign of the sea change under way in Afghanistan. Women returned for the first time in five years to their jobs at the Kabul office of the U.N. Refugee Agency UNHCR. The women had been barred from the U.N. Commission for Refugees Office in Afghan Capital, since 1996 when the Taliban came to power. While they were initially allowed to work in the field, they were barred in 1999 from doing any work at all and have since spent most of their time confined to their homes.

As the Taliban rulers were loosing their grip, the U.N. has asked the Northern Alliance to take special measures to protect the Buddhist statues that had escaped the Taliban destruction in the Central Afghan province of Bamiyan.

Five years after its shut down, the Indian mission in Afghanistan, an Indian Air Force IL-76 landed at the Bagram air base in Afghanistan on the morning of twentyfirst November, 2001 to express solidarity with the Afghan people after the ouster of the Taliban regime.

In order to have peace and security and a Government of National unity in the country so that the people of Afghanistan do not face hardship and problems. Rabbani expressed his willingness to step down.

Towards lasting political stability in Afghanistan, a historic conference was convened in Bonn, Germany on twentyseventh, November, 2001 where a total of twentyfive delegates took part in the talks including several from the mainly ethnic Tajik and Uzbek, North Alliance, the ethnic Hazara community as well as supporters of the former Afghan King, Mohammad Zahir Shah.

After hectic parleys between different factions of Afghanistan for eight days, four Afghans signed a pact under the auspices of the United Nations to create a new administration headed by an anti-Taliban battlefield commander, concluding a historic agreement aimed at restoring peace and stability to the war ravaged nation. Hamid Karzai, a moderate Muslim whose fighters were part of the campaign to push out the Taliban from their last strong hold in Kandahar was chosen to head the interim administration to replace the Taliban rule after the Northern Alliance took control of most of the country.

The U.N.Security Council authorized Britain for organization and command of multinational force to protect the Afghan capital of Kabul. Britain was the obvious choice because it could deploy troops quickly and has experience in leading a multinational force such as commanding the U.N. troops in Bosnia.

Hamid Karzai who is leading the Afghanistan government after fall of the Taliban desired the U.S. not to "walk away from Afghanistan" and pledged his support to the U.S. in the cause of either to capture or kill members of Laden's Al-Qaeda net-work. He termed Mullah Mohammad Omar, a fugitive, a criminal who committed crimes and killed thousands of people and brought the terrorists to Afghanistan. The U.N.Security Council on the 21st of December 2001 authorized an international force to help peace in Afghanistan capital of Kabul with Britain leading the troops and the U.S. prepared to rescue them in the emergency. A vanguard of some two hundred and fifty soliders were deployed around Kabul on the 22nd December when the country's new interim government with Hamid Karzai as Prime Minister sworned.

After driving out the Taliban, Hamid Karzai was sworn in on 23rd December 2001 as leader of Afghanistan with 29 other members of the cabinet including two women. The U.N. delegates, diplomats and a top U.S. General gathered to witness an end to war. Britain reopened its embassy in Kabul after twelve years on 23rd December,. India was represented by its Foreign Minister on this occasion.

After a day of fanfare, hugs and speeches, the Afghan new leader, Hamid Karzai, got down to the job of rebuilding his shattered land with a meeting of his cabinet, as the U.S. war planes still patrolling the skies, he appointed, ethnic Uzbek war-lord, Abdul Rashid Dostu as Deputy Defence Minister in his two-day old Government.

While the esrtwhile Taliban regime destroyed all musical instruments in the country labeling them as un-Islamic, the new Afghan interim Government has sent SOS to India for despatch of a set of musical instruments to compose the new National anthem. The new Government declared on 25th December that it will fight terrorism till its elimination from the World and resolved to frame a stringent anti-terrorism law with help from India and other countries.

Dr.Abdullah Abdullah, Foreign Minister of Afghanistan said that Afghanistan will allow the U.S. military forces to run a practically open-ended-compaign against terrorism on its territory. "We do not want to see the job half done. The objective is to fully eradicate terrorists" he said.

After years of working under cover or in exile, the Afghanistan actors have attempted to revive their art. Since the Taliban fled the city of Nou, twelve to thirteen male and female actors have returned to the vast but under-equipped premises of *Radio Afghanistan* which has become their main employer.

Afghanistan was demanding the U.S. to halt its bombing since almost all remaining border hideouts of the Taliban and Laden have been destroyed. The Deputy Defence Minister of the new Afghan Government said, "the Taliban cannot wage a war against us, but they can still create huge problems like committing acts of terrorism and kidnapping our people. They simply changed their turban color and melted into the population".

The British Government has deputed various regiments with equipment to set up the U.N. mandated International Security Assistance Force (ISAF) in Afghanistan.

Long excluded from Government, deprived of places of worship and exiled to far corners of the globe the Afgahnistan Sikh and Hindu minorities were yearning for peace after the dreaded Taliban regime has been ousted. In predominantly Muslim Afghanistan, Sikhs and Hindus share the same temples as well as many religious ceremonies.

An advance column of about fifty British troops drove into the Afghan capital, Kabul to take up peace keeping duties, the vanguard of international security force that was agreed with Afghanistan new rulers. Officials of the new Afghan interim Government and Britain were poring over the final wording of a formal agreement on the force authorized by the U.N.Security Council to fill the security vacuum in Afghanistan after the collapse of the Taliban. The peace-keeping force expected to number three thousand has been a source of disquiet for members of the Afghan administration.

Chairman of Afghanistan's interim Government Hamid Karzai desired the U.S. bombings of Afghanistan to continue until all terrorist activity was rooted out but also expressed concern about the mounting civilian causalities.

With large bands of the erstwhile Taliban still sheltered in Southern and Eastern Afghanistan, anti-Indian sentiments were still rife in Pashtun heart-land of Afghanistan and travel for any Indian in the region was almost a close brush with death.

Three Ministers in the Taliban regime deprived of power in November by the U.S. led compaign surrendered to the authorities, one by one along with the senior Talibans.

Hamid Karzai, the new leader of Afghanistan pledged to rid

his country of drug trafficking but said it would be difficult task without investment in the devastated agricultural economy.

With the Kabul Government pleading for 45 billion dollars to resurrect its devastated land, the U.S. looked beyond Afghanistan in its war on terrorism but still pressed with its destruction of remnant militant hideouts inside the country.

The Bush Administration prepared to release 221 million dollars in Afghan Government assets frozen in 1999 to Afghanistan's new cash straved administration. The assets which belong to Afghanistan's Central Bank were frozen by the Clinton administration in 1999 because of the Taliban's role in harbouring the Al-Qaeda militants linked to attacks the previous year on the U.S. Embassies in Kenya and Tanzania. Following the Taliban's ouster from power the United Nations lifted the international sanctions on the Afghan Central Bank clearing the way for the Treasury Department to release the assets.

Kabul's airport heavily damaged during the U.S. compaign in Afghanistan was officially reopened on sixteenth January 2002 after being cleared of bombs and mines starting a new era for Afghanistan. The U.S. Secretary of State, Colin Powell who arrived in Afghanistan on the Seventeenth of January assured that Washington would stand by the war-shattered country for a long time to come and planned a significant contribution for its reconstruction. He said that the U.S. military presence in Afghanistan was still necessary to uproot the remnants of Laden's Al-Qaeda network and the former ruling Taliban.

After six year of the Taliban rule, soccer team ran out on to Kandahar's Sports Stadium pitch on 17th January for the first 90 minutes game in the Southern City, since the austere, dictatorial theocracy fell to the U.S. bombs and fighters of the new, interim Government in December. Afghanistan has also returned to the Asain games in Pusan, South Korea in September,2002 after it was banned from the International Sports ever since the Taliban took over the country.

This time there was no blood underfoot. The players were allowed to wear shorts and the color red. They do not have to worry about the length of their hair or whether their beards are long enough.

Afghan's interim leader Hamid Karzai who had been to Japan on the 12th January to attend the international donor's conference after his talks with Saudi-Arabian leaders informed that Saudi Arabia had pledged an initial twenty million dollars in urgent aid for his shattered country.

The World came together on 21st January to pledge billions of dollars to rebuild Afghanistan whose interim Leader told an international conference that his country had known "nothing but disaster, war, brutality and deprivation. The U.S., Japan and Europe promised about 1.3 billion dollars more than the 2.6 billion dollars the aid pledged by the conference participants.

President Bush has made it clear, "that the U.S. will not abandon the people of Afghanistan". In Afghanistan men out number women. Still women advocates said that polygamy, which is permitted under traditional interpretations of Islam and is practised in most of the Muslim world, has increased in Afghanistan in the past decade or so. The renewed popularity of polygamy coincided with a broad erosion of women's rights under the post-Soviet regime of Mujahideen and particularly under the Taliban. Now Afghanistan has a new interim Government and is in the World's gaze. Therefore, many women's groups are lobbying for men to abandon polygamy just as they press women to shed their head to toe veils.

Polygamy may have made some sense at the time of the Prophet Mohammad but it has no place in modern Afghan's society. Muslim men are allowed four wives according to Koran. "The great Prophet Mohammad meant men to marry just not for sex and enjoyment but to take care of women who were suffering or widowed with many children". Prophet Mohammad married a second bride of seventeen years old, when he was fiftyfour year old.

The U.N. Secretary General, Kafi Annan arrived in

Afghanistan on the 25th of January on a short visit to see what more the World Body could do for the devastated country. He was the latest lengthening list of high profile visitors whose trips reflected Afghanistan's emergence into the World community after years as pariah State. Interim Afghan leader Hamid Karzai was enveloped in an emotional embrace by his country's exile community on the 28th of January as he began his first official visit to the United States with a call for his countrymen to come home. "Without your cooperation we are not going to make it," Karzai told several thousand Afghans and Afghan Americans who come from throughout the region to see him at George Town University's McDonough Gymnasium. Karzai has presided over the official reopening of Afghanistan's Embassy here which was closed after the Taliban regime took over the Government in Kabul in 1996. Soon after reaching the Andrews Air Force base, he dropped his bags at Blair House and headed for a small mosque at the Mustafa centre in Annandale Va.

Hamid Karzai met President Bush on the day of his arrival to the U.S. Bush pledged to rebuild Afghanistan, which was ravaged by 23 years of war and rebellion. The President made it clear that he had not budged from his insistence that other Nations provide the troops for peace keeping force in Afghanistan despite Karzai's hope that the U.S. military would take part. "Better yet than peace keepers let's have Afghanistan have her own military" Bush said. The White House has also offered new details of the U.S. humanitarian assistance for Afghanistan, released assets that had been frozen during the Taliban rule and extended credit to encourage private investment.

Karzai was in the U.S. to thank the Bush administration for getting rid off the Taliban and to ask for help in rebuilding the battered Afghanistan. Karzai literally got a red carpet welcome to Washington. He met President Bush and the top U.S. leaders to plead for more assistance and, in an emotional moment met with the Afghan expatriates. In his green robe and with his soft spoken humble manner and a chiseled face, he made a handsome figure and was most sought after guest on every television and radio show.

Hours before Bush's speech, Karzai visited the State Department for a ceremony officially announcing a two hundred and ninety-six million dollars U.S. aid and package and an immediate infusion of fifteen million dollars for quick start projects in education and agriculture. This will include 6.5 million dollars to print and distribute nearly ten million science, maths and other text books in time for the opening day of schools along with black boards and other school supplies. Karzai left Washington with the U.S. pledge to help and train a new Afghan army and police force as well reconstruction aid. In his first visit to Islamabad, since he assumed power, Karzai pledged to work for the release of what he called "good" Pakistanis captured along side the Taliban troops. Both countries have also vowed to rejuvenate strong brotherly relations based on mutual respect and trust while building Afghanistan on principles of sovereign equality, non-interference and mutual interest without allowing each others country to be used against the interest of either country.

On 16th December, 2002, India opened consulates in Kandahar, a former stronghold of the Taliban and Jalalabad taking such offices to four besides its embassy in Kabul. The two consulates in Herat and Mazar-e-Sharif have become functional with effect from 11th August,2002.

24

MYSTERY SURROUNDING LADEN'S ARREST

Even after thirty long months of frantic search by the troops of the US and Northern Alliance the where abouts of Bin Laden are not known. Abu Mohammed Al-Ablaj in an e-mail interview published by a Maiallah, a Saudi owned weekly stated in the second week of September, 2003 that the "Al Queda is every where around the World and in strength and Bin Laden is running the terror War against the United States from a cave, the same cave from where the orders went out to destroy the citadel of the Pentagon and which the Pentagon has not been able to destroy".

"Abu Abdullah Bin Laden enjoys full freedom of movement. He directs the fighting against the evil administration in Satan's black house from his cave".

"He wears to die fighting for God. Like any Mujahedeen, he cannot imagine dying in his bed", added al-Ablaj.

Pakistan President Pervez Musharaff who once said Laden is most likely dead because he has not been able to get treatment for his kidney disease" changed his view while giving interview to ABC news on 22nd September 2003. He admitted Laden is alive and may be hiding in Pakistan even as he vowed not to allow resurgence of the Al-queda.

"I think he's on the run, Al-Queda is on the run. Taliban supporters are on the run", said Musharraf. He said the terrorist master-mind could be in Pakistan or even hiding in Afghanistan and could be shifting places. "I am very sure, reasonably sure, that he is shifting places. He is not at one location and so we need to counter a strategic threat developing". Musharraf said. Elaborating, he said the strategic threat could be the unison of the al-Queda with Taliban supporters and with the dissenting moderates. "We will not allow that on our side. With each passing day, our intelligence set-up and the quick reaction force, effectiveness is improving and we are very sure that our side will be acting strongly, and there is no possibility of strategic build-up here", the Pakistan President said. He also said Pakistan needs more assistance from the US in fighting terrorism.

A leading London tabloid claimed on the 22nd February, 2004 that the World's most wanted terrorist Bin Laden has been tracked down and the SAS, British elite soldiers were poised to seize him in his secret mountain lair in Pakistan.

Working closely with the United State's, forces, the SAS have hemmed Laden into a remote mountain area measuring just 16 km wide in Pakistan bordering, Afghanistan, the *Sunday Express* claimed. The man behind the September 11 outrage is reportedly being guarded by only 50 of his most loyal supporters who have pledged to lay down their lives for him. The report quoted a US intelligence source saying, "He is boxed in". According to the report, SAS and the United States' special forces are awaiting orders to swoop on the world's most wanted man in the desolate Toba Kakar mountains in Pakistan's North-West frontier. The American military Chiefs are confident that Bin Laden - who is believed to be holed up with the Taliban leader Mullah Mohammed Omar - cannot escape. But British planners have warned against overconfidence. According to the report quoted to defence sources in London, the UK is reluctant to get drawn into a full-blown "Spring Offensive" to wipe out the ruminants of al-Qaeda, although US President George W. Bush favours the move as a boost to his re-election prospects in November.

Basing on the above reports Pakistan troops launched a fresh offensive in the last week of February, 2004 against Al-Qaeda and Taliban militants hiding in remote tribal areas near Afghan border. The Information Minister, Sheik Rahid Ahmed of Pakistan said the latest operation was launched near Wana, nearly 190 miles northeast of where Bin Laden was reported to be hiding. The operation came hours after President Bush vowed on 24th February to track down Al-qaeda militants. "We are on the hunt for Al-Qaeda", he told a meeting of U.S. Governors at the White House. He further stated "it requires all assets, intelligence assets and military assets, to chase them down and bring them to justice and we are going pretty good - better than pretty good". The operation also follows a visit to Pakistan in the month of January, 2004 by the CIA Director, George Tenet in which he is thought to have discussed the hunt for Bin Laden and al-Qaeda. Pakistan, a key ally in the U.S. led war on terror, has arrested more than 500 Al-qaeda suspects and handed them over to the U.S.

Security forces swooped on an area near the town of Wana 300 Kilometers West of the capital in a six-hour operation on the 24th of Feb. 2004 hunting for clues on the whereabouts of fugitive Al-Qaeda leader Bin Laden and his top lieutenants. Authorities pressed the suspects through the night, trying to determine why they are - and whether they had any links to Bin Laden. Among the 25 people caught are three Arab women and some other foreigners. The Interior Minister of Pakistan told that "it is always difficult to establish identity of the terrorists, especially if they are members of al-Qaeda, because they are well-trained and keep changing their statements".

On the 24th of February, 2004 the CIA, Director George Tenet said that despite strides made against al-Qaeda it remained, capable of conducting an attack on the scale of Sept. 11, 2001 and he warned of dangers from broader anti-American sentiment among Muslim extremists. "We are still at War", Tenet said at an annual senate intelligence committee hearing on worldwide threats. Al-

Qaeda remained committed to attacking the United States and its allies, he added.

Iran's State radio, quoting an unnamed source, said on 28th Feb. 2004 that Osama Bin Laden was captured in Pakistan "a long time ago", A Pakistan army spokesman denied he was captured. The report said that the US Defence Secretary Donald Rumsfeld's visit to the region was in connection with the arrest. The State radio said a reporter for its Pushtun Service in the northwestern Pakistani city of Peshawar "confirmed the news" that Bin Laden had been captured in a tribal region in Pakistan. He said the news was from "a very reliable source in Peshawar, Pakistan" but the source was not identified. Pakistani army spokesman Gen. Shaukat Sultan told the reporters that the report is completely untrue. "That information is a wrong", he said.

The Pakistan, Interior Minister, Makhdoom Syed Faisal Saleh Hayat stated on the 17th of March 2004 that Bin Laden 'cannot' be hiding in Pakistan because the Pakistani Military had "virtually sealed the border" with Afghanistan, He further, said that "we do not believe Laden is in Pakistan, because if he had been in Pakistan, certainly by now in view of the nature of the operations, which has been initiated and conducted over the past two years, certainly he would have been apprehended". The Minister said that Laden could be somewhere along the border belt, because it is a very long border of 2500 km in which they got most inhospitable terrain anywhere in the World.

The U.S. led forces, however, have launched a new operation across a broad area of the south and east of Afghanistan aimed at capturing top Al-Qaeda and the Taliban militants. The operation code named "Mountain Storm" was launched on the 7th of March 2004 and involved troops from the 13,500 strong U.S. - led forces backed by air support. Though, the U.S. led forces have launched new operations aimed at capturing al-Qaeda and the Taliban militants, Ayman al-Zawahri, who is the real brain behind Bin Laden, claimed to have purchased some ready-made nuclear weapons and suit case bombs on a Central Asian black market to destroy their enemies.

The U.S. President G.W. Bush said that after the capture of Saddam Hussain "good riddance". The world is better of without you Mr. Saddam Hussain. What would he say to the world if, Bin Laden is arrested or killed?

INDEX